RECALIBRATING
YOUR
RELATIONAL
IQ

DAVID S. JACQUES

GP

GODZCHILD PUBLICATIONS

Published by Godzchild Publications
a division of Godzchild, Inc.
22 Halleck St., Newark, NJ 07104
www.godzchildproductions.net

Printed in the United States of America 2017 - 1st Edition

Library of Congress Cataloging-in-Publications Data
On the Other Side of Barlow/Racha Barlow

ISBN-13 978-0692101551

1.Jacques, David 2.

2018

Cutting edge, creative, and captivating are just some of the ways to describe this literary masterpiece by Pastor David Jacques. As an accomplished Pastor and entrepreneur, Pastor Jacques has been fortunate to interact and interface with people from all walks of life. Hence, his spiritual and business-related experiences help to make him a reliable subject-matter expert worth listening to. Therefore, if you are looking for ways to increase your own relational IQ or strengthen your team, this book is a must read!

Emory Berry, D.Min
Greenforest Community Baptist Church

It can be said that the quality of our lives is greatly determined by who is in it. In this unique and insightful work, David Jacques provides practical principles to help others understand the power of placement. We can't always control who is in our lives, but we can control where we put them. This book is an amazing tool that will help you determine who goes where.

Dharius Daniels, D.Min
Lead Pastor, Change Church
Author, RePresent Jesus

I am honored to be among the first to read this book. While relationships are essential, relationships are built on our deepest areas of vulnerabilities.

David Jaques has masterfully illustrated the value of both relationships and the boundaries necessary to protect them. I have found David to be an authentic friend and a brother beloved. His heart for God, his family, his congregation and his community sets him apart as a shepherd and leader.

I recommend this book to both singles and married people as I believe it is enlightening, encouraging and edifying.

Timothy Jones, D. Min
Peaceful Rest Baptist Church
Shreveport, LA

DEDICATION

I would like to dedicate Recalibrating Your Relational IQ to a host of folks, first to my wife, Karen, who encouraged me to write, particularly this book. Along with my wife, I dedicated this book my four amazing children: David, Destini, Desiree, and Deven. My beloved parents Saint Jean and Marie Jacques I love you both eternally. To my siblings Piccard and Emmanuelle. To my mother and father-in-law, Jeannot and Marie Abraham, thank you for your support. My brothers and sisters in law. To The Kingdom Church-thank you for allowing me to grow before you and grow into maturity. To many of the friends that have encouraged me along the way. Finally, to my Pastors, Dr. R.A. Vernon and Lady Vernon, you continue to inspire me towards greatness.

Contact page
Pastor David S. Jacques
1400 N. Nowell St Orlando, FL 32808

C^{TABLE OF}ontents

It's important to define every relationship—to establish, provide, and respect the boundaries that determine the kind of relationships you want to have with those you interact with.

As someone with authority and popularity, my time and my word are two commodities I can't afford to misuse.

Through trial and error, I learned to set boundaries early and thoroughly with those I interact with. I frame every relationship with care. For example, A fellow preacher is a contemporary, but not a friend. My members are my supporters, but not my friends. I love them, they pay my bills, but I have a clear boundary that contextualizes our connection.

My wife, on the other hand, is my friend, but not my member, as she often reminds me.

Every relationship deserves and needs designation, for the benefit of all parties involved. From your spouse to your social acquaintances, where there is obscurity or ambiguity, there will almost certainly be incongruity, and the health of your relationships will improve or decline based on how well you're able to express and maintain your boundaries.

After all, lack of definition can lead to destruction if someone oversteps a boundary because they have some quixotic expectation based on an erroneous estimation of their place in your life.

That's where Pastor David's first work becomes an indispensable resource. He offers clear-cut instructions on how to traverse even the rockiest relational terrain.

If you've ever had trouble defining, preserving, or recognizing boundaries; or perhaps you've done a respectable job with setting boundaries for the most part, but need to adjust or address behaviors in one particular relationship that you sense is unhealthy, Recalibrating Your Relational IQ, is the book that is going to help you reset your relationships, once and for all.

R. A. Vernon, D.Min.

CHAPTER 1

RELATIONAL BOUNDARIES

I n the United States, the Department of Transportation was established by an act of Congress on October 15, 1966. The mission of the department is to "serve the United States by ensuring a fast, safe, efficient, accessible, and convenient transportation system that meets our vital national interests and enhances the quality of life of the American people, today and into the future." It is this department that oversees, designs, and manages pavement markings that we see on every paved road in the U.S. The pavement markings were created to convey messages to roadway users. They indicate which part of the road to use, and they protect both drivers and pedestrians from vehicular accidents. The yellow lines on the road separate traffic flow in opposite directions. A dashed yellow line indicates that passing is allowed. White lines, however, separate lanes for which travel is in the same direction. A double white line indicates that lane changes are prohibited, a single white line indicates that lane changes are discouraged, and a dashed white line indicates that lane changes are allowed. Imagine, for a moment, what it would be like to drive in the U.S. without pavement markings on the road? Since these markings are seen everywhere, we often take them for granted, but these yellow and white lines provide boundaries for us. They alert us to potentially hazardous conditions, and they forewarn us about the road changes ahead. Without these boundaries, we would run the risk of causing harm to ourselves, or causing harm to others. The same is true with relational boundaries.

Having clear relational boundaries is essential to having a balanced, healthy lifestyle. A boundary is a personal line that marks who we are and what we will do. Boundaries define us. Boundaries protect us. Boundaries guide us. Boundaries impact every area of our lives. Without boundaries, individuals cannot be held accountable for their actions. Without boundaries, people do not know what they can do or cannot do to you or with you. If you don't have boundaries—be they physical, mental, spiritual, or otherwise—you are in trouble.

Mental boundaries give us the freedom to have our own thoughts. Emotional boundaries help us to deal with our true feelings. They also help us to disengage from the harmful and manipulative actions of others. Spiritual boundaries help us to distinguish God's will from our human wants. When we embrace our spiritual boundaries, our awe for the Creator is renewed. It is absolutely possible to have a mental, emotional, and spiritual boundary, and still be open and loving. In fact, having those kinds of boundaries helps to ensure openness to the world and to the relationships you hold dear. If you've ever owned a home that is situated near another home, I'm sure you know the importance of a land survey. In simple terms, a land survey is a graphic depiction of a property, much like a map, that outlines its legal boundaries and features. The survey lays out the exact dimensions of a property so that outsiders cannot build on land that belongs to you. In the same way, boundaries show us where to build. They demarcate the safe and unsafe points of a relationship, and help to make sure that everyone on your proverbial property and everyone on your proverbial road, is traveling in the same direction as you.

EVERY RELATIONSHIP NEEDS BOUNDARIES

Every relationship needs boundaries. Now, when I speak of relationships, I am not only talking about the romantic relationship between a husband and wife. I am talking about every interpersonal exchange that can happen between two or more people. We have relationships with people with whom we work and worship, we have relationships with friends and associates, and we have relationships with strangers and enemies. Whether someone is your best friend, your colleague, or your associate, the designation doesn't diminish the reality. All of these are kinds of relationships. As such, each relationship needs to define its boundaries so that nothing is assumed and everyone can have a balanced, healthy lifestyle.

You cannot hold people accountable to unexpressed expectations. Boundaries are not organically assumed, they must be intentionally communicated. If you don't like to be called by the nickname of your past, you need to express that to others because people don't know what you don't tell them. If they hear someone else calling you by your childhood nickname, they may follow suit, assuming it is a term of endearment. But when you communicate your boundary from inception, then other people with whom you have relationship are clear about your desires and dissatisfactions—and if they are in violation of said boundaries, they know it and you know it.

Boundaries should be created before an infraction occurs, but more often than not, boundaries are created after someone violates your spoken or unspoken expectations. So, if someone oversteps a boundary with your family, yet they still seek help from you, it is appropriate to create another boundary with that person. Even if the person is in your family, you need to say something like, "Cousin, friend, co-worker...I value you and I love you, but if helping you will hurt my family, then I have to stop helping you." If the behavior continues, then an announcement must take place: *I can no longer help you. You have continued to hurt my family.* The announcement creates the boundary. Your commitment to your announcement creates accountability. Now that you have articulated your actions, you have saved yourself and others from unnecessary offense. But most times, people are too passive-aggressive to be honest with themselves and with others about the violation of boundaries. Normally, we shut down. We ignore. We hide. Or, we overcompensate by projecting our offense onto innocent bystanders. Healthy boundaries require adult decisions. It always helps to tell others the truth, even when the truth is hard to tell. This will save you unnecessary stress and aggravation in the end.

BOUNDARIES IN SCRIPTURE

And the Lord God commanded the man, "You are free to eat from any tree in the garden; but you must not eat from the tree of the knowledge of good and evil, for when you eat from it you will certainly die."

–Genesis 2:16-17

From the beginning of creation, boundaries have always been a part of God's plan for healthy relationships. God's first conversation with Adam begins with God saying something like this: *Listen Adam, you can do whatever you want in this field and you can have as much fun as you want. If you desire to do it, you can do it. Have at it! But what you cannot do is touch this particular tree because if you touch this tree, you will venture outside of the relational*

6

boundary that I have set up for us. And I want to keep this relationship good between you and me, so I'm going to tell you upfront what my expectations are. If you happen to do anything different from my articulated expectations, then you can't be offended by the consequences that will ensue as a result of you stepping outside of the boundary markers I have designed.

We all know what happens verses later. Adam violates those boundaries and eats what God says do not eat, but Adam and God aren't the only two entities in this scene that have to adhere to boundaries. Adam is surrounded by animals in the garden. He has been given jurisdiction by God to oversee, manage, and name the animals. But just because he's around them doesn't mean he is equal to them. A boundary is set between Adam and the animals the same way a boundary was set between the Creator and his creation. If we glean lessons from Adam's story, we will learn how to lead others around us without lowering our standards in order to win them toward us. Just because everyone else curses on your job, doesn't mean you need to lower your conversational standards in order to be liked by them. But if you don't set boundaries in the beginning by politely asking your co-workers not to curse around you, then it will be very difficult not to conform to the patterns they have set.

Before I began pastoring, I worked for Enterprise. One of my co-workers loved to scream at everyone. He didn't have a normal talking tone. Whenever he spoke to people, he would yell at the top of his lungs. This caused for a hostile work environment, and while he had not yelled at me, I knew his tone would cause irreparable damage if he tried that on me. So, to secure my witness as a Christian and to maintain my employee status at Enterprise, I decided to have a pre-emptive conversation with my co-worker. I invited him into the office, and after the door was closed, I kindly expressed these words to him, "You know, I've never had an altercation with you but I just want to share my heart so that I can be a productive employee. I do not work well with people who scream at me, and I've noticed that you scream at everyone else. If that is how you choose to relate to others, that's fine. But as for me, that's not going to work." I set the boundary upfront. I let him know before matters exacerbated into an altercation, what the consequence of said behavior would be if he overstepped those boundaries. Suffice it to say, I never had a problem with that co-worker.

God set boundaries with Adam beforehand. Adam could not say he was surprised or shocked by the resulting consequences of his actions because boundaries pronounce penalties. Boundaries will not eliminate the relationship but, if violated, boundaries will adjust the relationship. In Genesis, Adam's violation caused a separation. Because he ate from the tree God said do not eat from, he was suspended from the garden but not eliminated by God. In the same way, sometimes boundaries will cause separation for the sake of your mental preservation. It may hurt you to set that boundary. It may hurt you to distance yourself from someone you love (I'm sure God was just as hurt to see Adam removed from Garden as Adam was to be removed), but in the end, your mental stability and sanity are more important.

All of us have a family member whom we love dearly but we don't trust. Perhaps you, like me, have a thief in the family who comes over to eat, and leaves with a phone, a purse, or a ring that doesn't belong to them. The fact that they are family will never change. But how you relate to that family member depends on the boundaries you set. An honest boundary may sound like a conversation that begins in this way, "Look cousin, I love you man but every time you come over, something goes missing from the house. Now I'm not accusing you of stealing, but I am saying that it's missing." Instead of deciding never to deal with your cousin again, a healthier (biblical) boundary might be that you will visit your cousin's house from now on instead of inviting him over to your house. That way, if he steals from himself, it doesn't directly affect you! When you set the right boundary, you can still maintain the relationship. The key is to remove all the parts that make the relationship less fruitful. Most people discard the entire relationship instead of discerning which parts of the relationship are unhealthy. Proper boundaries help you to "eat the meat but throw out the bone."

EAT THE MEAT, THROW OUT THE BONE

I love my mother more than life itself, but my mom can't keep a secret. She just can't. If somebody paid her to keep a secret, she would tell who paid her, how much, and where they got the money from. One time, my brother told my mother he was going to propose to his girlfriend, and my mom decided to tell his girlfriend (now wife), "You know… my son said he's going to give you something special real soon; so, you need to be prepared when he gives it to you."

On another occasion, I stopped by mom's house and said, "Mom, Karen is pregnant but please don't tell anyone." My mom responded, "Oh baby! I'd never tell your secrets...never." But the moment I shut the door, she called her friend and said, "Sister, my son come over. He tell me he having a baby. Don't tell anybody, ok? Just me and you." But I understand my mother, so I don't judge her or disown her. My mother is from Haiti, and if you know anything about islanders, you know they love to hold a lot of conversation. Conversation about anything and everything! So, my mom loves to talk. She tells people's secrets, and that's a bad thing. But she also talks to God, which is a good thing. For the last 40 years, every Saturday, my mother has led prayer. She is a prayer warrior who knows the power of intercession. She has seen God do the miraculous. My life is a testament to those miracles. My mother had me when she was 46 years old. God spoke to her in a dream and told her that her child was going to be a pastor. And from the time I came out of the womb, all I've ever wanted to be was a pastor. Her prayers helped guide my purpose. Without her talking to God, she wouldn't have been able to mold me into the person I am today.

If your mom was like my mom, I'm sure you might be tempted to cut off the relationship or limit your visits to holidays and birthdays. But to protect our relationship, I've learned not to share anything that doesn't need to be shared prematurely. Furthermore, to keep myself from getting mad at my mom, I control what I say, how I say it and when I say it. Proper boundaries will save the meat of the relationship while simultaneously allowing you to throw away the bone.

Is your dad always negative? Then don't bring him good news that he can turn into bad news. Does your friend embarrass you in public? Then don't put yourself in a predicament that makes you uncomfortable. Create spaces where you feel safe. I have a lot of "hothead" friends. I know they have tempers so I shy away from vacation trips to Miami or New York. One time I took a hothead friend of mine to NY, and he started fighting with everybody! He was mad that everyone kept bumping into him, but I think he forgot that 8.5 million people live in NYC. Truthfully, this was my fault though. I knew he wouldn't be successful navigating through this kind of environment, and it's not because he's a bad person. Like my other friend who doesn't pay anyone back, I've had to learn how to establish boundaries that keep them from seeing the worst part of themselves. Boundaries help me to value the friend versus losing the friendship. You too can have this kind of freedom if you are willing to make some minor relational adjustments.

INITIAL CONTACT

Now the serpent was more crafty than any of the wild animals the Lord God had made. He said to the woman, "Did God really say, 'You must not eat from any tree in the garden'?" The woman said to the serpent, "We may eat fruit from the trees in the garden, but God did say, 'You must not eat fruit from the tree that is in the middle of the garden, and you must not touch it, or you will die.'" "You will not certainly die," the serpent said to the woman. "For God knows that when you eat from it your eyes will be opened, and you will be like God, knowing good and evil."

–Genesis 3:1-4

How does one create boundaries and relate to people whom they meet for the first time? Short Answer: Ask more questions than you answer. When the serpent greets Eve in the Garden, this is their first interaction.

You would think Eve's first question would be, "Who are you," or "Where did you come from?" But she doesn't ask the right questions. Instead, she answers the antagonist without vetting the voice. She is distracted by excitement. She is overwhelmed by curiosity. Immediately, she engages an outsider and makes him privy to inside information. Most of us are a lot like Eve. When we meet people for the first time, we are intoxicated by excitement or curiosity. Especially in romantic situations, we tend to give too much of ourselves too quickly, and within the first few conversations, we let our guard down. Even in business and in ministry, this principle still applies. Often when an aspirant creative or a hopeful mentee meets someone of significance in their field or in the world, they formulate a preconceived ideology regarding who they might become in relationship to this great influencer. As mentee, we assume this relationship is the gateway into the next opportunity. But this person has not promised to do anything for us yet. Nevertheless, we assign labels of expectation upon them. When they don't do what we expected them to do, we become frustrated and disappointed. In so doing, we set ourselves up for failure because we had an unexpressed expectation and an undefined boundary. In short, we become entitled. And whenever expectation is coupled with entitlement, offense is inevitable.

Whenever you encounter someone for the first time, ask more questions than you answer so you are not hurt by over-expectation. When the serpent converses with Eve, he uses his words to stroke her ego. When you eat of this tree, you will be wise and you will be smart like God. But people who don't know who they are can't tell you who you are. If Eve had truly embraced who she was, she wouldn't have allowed the enemy to talk her out of her garden. In the same way, when we don't know who we are, we often turn to other people to fill our void. We turn to others for affirmation, and in the end, we lose our center. I heard it once said this way, "If you live for the applause of man, then you'll die when they are silent." In other words, if people (who don't know you) have to affirm you in order for you to feel significant, then you don't just have a boundary issue…you have an identity issue.

When someone doesn't know who they are, they become vulnerable to the opinions of others around them, even if those opinions are unwarranted, unbiblical and inaccurate. Isn't it funny, that the most directionless people are also those who try to give the most direction? Be careful, as you learn to implement boundaries, that you do not allow others to project their baggage or brokenness onto you. Parents do it to their children all of the time. If a parent doesn't like someone, then they will tell their child about their dislike and then expect their child not to like that person simply because the parent doesn't like them. If a certain career path doesn't pay a hefty salary, sometimes parents will try to discourage their child from studying in that field because they are projecting their ideas of success onto their children. But unlike the parent-child relationship, the serpent was a complete stranger to Eve, and yet, he still had significant influence over her decision-making abilities. Eve believed someone she had just met over someone she had been with all along. What Eve needed was a tutorial on relational boundaries with strangers and first-time engagers. That is the purpose of this book.

As we further unpack the subject of boundaries in the chapters to come, we will examine how to live a healthy life with every relationship you encounter, so that the pavement marking you establish in life, will protect you and guide you on the road toward destiny.

CHAPTER 2

RELATIONAL PLACEMENT

In this fast-paced, technologically savvy, social media world, it is my strong opinion that the word 'friend' has been thrown around too casually. Facebook calls everyone who views your profile a "friend." Instagram calls everyone who sees your pictures a follower, and Twitter calls everyone who likes your quotes a follower. But the truth is, every follower is not a friend, and every friend on Facebook is not a friend in life. We know this cognitively, but we live like this fact isn't true in actuality. Sometimes, our language betrays our logic. Most people call an associate a friend. We call work colleagues our friends, and even in church, we assume that just because they attend our church or serve on the same ministry team as us, they are our friend. But allow me to burst your proverbial bubble with this clarifying truth: half of these people are not your friend. At best, this is a transactional relationship. At worst, this is a foe dressed up in friendly clothing.

Yes, I said it. A transactional relationship is a relationship between two individuals who both have an agenda, an expectation, and a motive. Your realtor is not your friend. Sure, she helped you purchase your first home, but she is not your friend. Let's tell the truth. She is a lovable consultant with an effervescent personality. You are her client. You are her customer. Her motive is to persuade you to purchase property. When you purchase, she profits. If you don't, the relationship ends. After all of the small-talk, check-ins, and courteous platitudes, a check will be given or received. Why? Because this is a transactional relationship.

Your barber is not your friend. Sure, you've gone to him for ten years, and to be fair, if you've had the same barber for any consistent number of years, the relationship may have graduated to friendship. But when it started, it was a transactional relationship. This was work-for-hire, and if he messed up your hairline, or if she messed up your perm, you terminated the business transaction immediately (sometimes without an announcement).

Even though your barber or beautician talks with you about life, love, and gossip while doing your hair, after the razor has been applied to your beard, and after the hairspray has been applied to your hair, chances are, your barber is not going to call you tomorrow to see if you need a ride to work. So, go ahead and tell your beautician all your business—*I hate my husband. My boss gets on my nerves. My ex just hit the lottery*—you can tell him or her all your business if you want to, but you can't be upset if they mishandle your heart, mismanage your issues, or break your confidentiality. She was hired to do one thing—to clip your split ends, not to give you a therapy session. This is a transactional relationship.

I'm sure you love your boss. I'm sure you appreciate and value their wisdom and experience. I'm sure they love you. But, be clear: your boss is not your friend. Your boss can never really be your true friend because your relationship with that boss is predicated on your check arriving safely into your checking account, every 1st and 15th of the month. Let the check not show up after a few pay periods, and see if that friendship still remains. Will you still, in the name of friendship, come to work and slave over a hot stove, or meddle through difficult paperwork, or teach those children without a check? Don't get it twisted. Your boss is not your bestie. Your boss is your supervisor. He or she is responsible for evaluating, training, and compensating you for services rendered.

It's O.K. Call them whatever you'd like to call them. But make sure you are aware of what you mean when you call someone a friend. In other words, don't confuse transactional relationships with real relationships. Knowing the difference is crucial to your relational IQ because relationship categorization is all about proper placement. In order to do relationships right, you need to stop categorizing people wrong. Mature individuals place people where they belong, instead of assigning a role to them that is incommensurate with what they actually bring to the table. Tell the truth. This was work-for-hire. Tell the truth. He was a rebound to help you get over your ex. Tell the truth. She only wanted to have lunch with you to see if you could help her with her résumé. The more honest you are with yourself about who someone is and who someone is not, the more forthright you will be with your true friends.

WHAT IS A FRIEND?—FRIENDSHIP 101

A friend loves at all times, and a brother is born for a time of adversity.

– Proverbs 17:17

Let's begin with the basics. I'd like to call this section Friendship 101. What is a friend? According to the Bible, the Greek word for friend is *philos,* which means, "someone dearly loved or prized in a personal (and sometimes intimate) way." A friend is a trusted confidant. A friend is one who is held dear in a close bond of personal affection. Let's unpack some of these definitions for a moment. A friend is not just dearly loved; a friend is a prized possession. A prize is something you appreciate. A prize is a gift that most times, you don't deserve. If you don't value the prize, or if you misuse that prize, over time, its value will depreciate. In the same way, friends should be valued, and whatever you value…will appreciate. Friends should be celebrated. People should know who your friends are, and you should regularly tell them how much they mean to you. The worst thing you could ever do is lose a true friend because you forgot to value you them for who they really are.

As a prize, friends deserve respect. If you say something behind your friend's back, then you should respect the relationship enough to say it in front of their face. Friends don't let friends go through dark seasons alone. Friends will be there with you through the thick and the thin. Friends are with you on the mountain and the valley. Friends will turn the world upside down to make sure you are safe, secure, and whole. Friends are trusted confidants, and trust doesn't happen overnight. In order for someone to become your friend, they must stand the test of time. Friends keep your secrets. Friends don't expose you to others. Friends know how to maneuver between circles. So if your friend has a mutual associate, and that associate knows you, a true friend won't spill the beans to the associate simply because you all know each other. Friends manage their relationships in a mature manner. They are not perfect, but they can be trusted. If you're trying to figure out whether or not someone is your friend, ask yourself, "Can they be trusted? Has their trust been proven? Can they hold what you share with them without telling anyone else?"

Of course, there are exceptions to every rule. So, depending on the nature of your secret, friends know when a secret is too dangerous to keep to themselves. If you are being abused or if you want to take your life, friends may risk the possibility of disappointment from you in order to save you from yourself. But, only in matters of extreme conflict will friends share the details of your heart with others. Even then, if he or she is your friend, they will tell you what they said and to whom they said it.

A friend loves at all times. A friend is with you in rehab. A friend is with you if you relapse. A friend is with you when you give your life to Christ. A friend is with you if you decide to turn away. A friend does not necessarily condone every decision you make, but a friend will always be there to help you if you want their help. A true friend doesn't impose. A true friend just shows up. A true friend doesn't need to know what to say. Sometimes, their mere presence is enough to help you cope through difficult seasons.

EVERYBODY AIN'T YOUR BFF

Be careful who you call your BFF or your bestie. These designations are cute ascriptions that we apply to people to whom we feel close, but a true best friend isn't determined by good times. A true best friend is determined through difficult times. Let's be honest. Everybody loves you when times are good. Who wouldn't want to be your friend if you hit the lottery today? Who wouldn't want to be your friend if you're on the red carpet accepting awards and taking pictures on the cover of popular magazines. Those are the good times. When the baby is first born, when the marriage is sizzling hot, when the money is in the bank, and when food is on the table. When the boss gives you a promotion, or when you step out and start your own business. When life is good and all is well, many people will magnetize to the greatness they see in an attempt to get what they want from you. But a true friend has endured tribulation with you. A real friend has disagreed with you, disliked you for something you did or said, but showed up in the morning to work it out. A best friend must be proven. A best friend has seen me at my worst, and loves me enough to stay. A best friend isn't someone you speak to everyday necessarily. But the weight of their presence is felt when you need them the most.

Nowadays, this millennial generation and millennial culture is so twisted. Even if we don't fall within the age bracket of the typical millennial, we still participate in millennial behavior, especially in our friendships. In this day and age, we will throw away an 8 year tried-and-true-friendship all because we found a new group of people at our new job. In this day and age, if our tax bracket changes and we start making a few more dollars, we will drop our childhood friends for some "uppity friends," thinking that a tax bracket is the way you decide who deserves to be close to you. But the islanders would say this, "It's better to keep an old pot than to get a new one." By that they mean, think twice before you throw away that which is trustworthy for somebody new. Everything that glitters isn't gold. Everything that shines isn't a diamond. Every grass field isn't green, and if it's too green, it's artificial.

Every friendship will endure a difficult season. Every friendship will hit a moment where you think to yourself, "I can't stand you." If your friend hasn't gotten on your nerves one good time yet, then it's not a friendship. You two are just acquaintances. You may be married with children, but if they haven't worn out your patience to the point that you wanted to argue, yell, or fight (maybe one of these, or all three!) then they are just an acquaintance. The beauty of true friendship is longevity.

No matter what, the bond is tight because I know you will be there for me even if we disagree. We may see politics differently, but you're my friend. We may date different people, but you are my friend. We may worship at different churches and embrace a different religion altogether, but you are my friend. If you have a good friend, appreciate him or her. It's a bad thing to get rid of good people. Even if the relationship has had to shift because of relocation, marriage, or children, keep the relationship. Even if they overstepped a boundary, don't eliminate the relationship…just reclassify them. A friend loves at all times. Good times. Bad Times. Sunny Times. Stormy Times. All times…is all times.

THE DANGER OF BURNING BRIDGES

Every friendship will not last a lifetime. Some friends are in your life for a season. Some friends are in your life for a reason. And some friends are in your life for a lifetime. Your job is to discern who is in your life for what purpose, and then to water the garden of that relationship until it's time to move on. But be careful, even as you identify those "seasonal friendships," not to burn a bridge too soon. If you burn a bridge simply because you don't like someone, you never know when you might need to cross that bridge again later. Many of us know what it's like to burn a bridge or to have a bridge burned by someone else. We have cut off or been cut off, and then, ten years later, when we are praying for God to open a door, we realize that it can't happen because the bridge we needed to cross over, has been compromised.

Someone reading this section may be adamantly disagreeing with me because in your mind, God holds the key to every door; and in part that's true. But God entrusts people to hold the key that He has designed for the door He's predestined for you to walk through. Because God uses people, what you do to others can directly or indirectly affect you. This is why Scripture admonishes us to "live peaceably with all men." No, we don't have to go out to eat every day, and no we don't have to be best friends. But I never know when God will tell me to go back to a person from my past in order to gain access to my future. So I must conduct myself in a way that sees everyone as an angel unaware. Everyone has the potential to be a person to whom God has given a key, for me and my family to enter into our next chapter. How you handle your bridges will determine whether you will enter into your doors.

THE ULTIMATE SACRIFICE

Greater love has no one than this: to lay down one's life for one's friends.

¬John 15:13

The supreme duty of a friend is sacrifice. The supreme call of a true friend is to sacrifice for his or her friend in order to ensure that their friend is secure. True friends will sacrifice their security for your success. True friends have this mindset—if I have to suffer so you can excel, I am willing to do that because I hold you dear as my prized possession. I know you have 5,000 friends on Facebook, but how many people in your life are willing to sacrifice for you? How many friends are willing to inconvenience themselves (for a day) in order to see you thrive for a lifetime? This is what it means to be a lifetime friend. A lifetime friend is not determined by how much money one has in the bank. A lifetime friend is determined by how much one is willing to sacrifice for his friendship. Jesus was the greatest example of sacrifice. His willful decision to lay down his life for us, is the best picture of pure, loving, selfless friendship. Real friends don't think twice about calling each other when they are in a bind. If I am stranded at 3am, I call my real friends. If I'm hesitating to call you because I don't want to bother you, we aren't real friends. If I'm thinking twice about how this call might mess up your day tomorrow, we aren't real friends. And if you aren't willing to get up and come get me at 3am, we aren't real friends. Godly, biblical friendship is reciprocal. One never gives more than the other, even if what they give each other is different in material value. The quality is nevertheless the same. Real friends will fight today and forgive tomorrow. Real friends will sacrifice sleep in order to make you smile. This is the kind of friend who loves at all times. If the people you call on the most aren't willing to do this, you need to reclassify them. They may not be bad people, but they are certainly not your friend.

F.R.I.E.N.D.

A few years ago, I created this acronym that I use to define the true value of a God-ordained friend. I recommend this acronym as a checklist to elevate or eliminate certain individuals from your life this year.

F – a true friend will **FIGHT** for you. A true friend will defend you in your absence. A true friend will not just fight for you, but they will fight with you. In a true friend's mine, your friends are their friends, and your enemies are their enemies. If a true friend sees you getting jumped, they are automatically going to join the fight to help you. Pay attention to people who will watch you get bullied from the sideline and do nothing. Whether you are being physically bullied, emotionally bullied, or verbally bullied, the silence of the spectator screams louder than the punches of the participator.

R – a true friend will **RESPECT** you. A respectful friend may not agree with everything you do or say, but they honor you enough to tell you the truth. A true friend will not allow people on the outside to appreciate you more than the people on the inside. If your spouse is your friend, then you will respect them. If your spouse is just a romantic partner, then you will only love them as long as they are giving you what you want. Have you ever met a couple who had high accolades but low respect? The man gets out of the car without acknowledging, helping, or assisting his wife. The woman talks down about the man every time she gets an opportunity to disparage him. Respect says, "Even though I know your valleys, I will only promote your mountains. No one will ever see me humiliate you publicly. No one will ever say that I dishonored our relationship because of a disagreement." As friend, we honor one another—in each other's presence, and away from one another. No matter the price, respect is a non-negotiable.

I – a true friend will **INCLUDE** you. Have you ever met someone who makes decisions for whole groups of people without asking them for their input? Have you ever met someone who assumes that because they know you, they can decide for you? A true friend will not assume they know you, even though they know you well. Instead, they will include you in decisions. They will include you in their lives. They will invite you to be a part of their monumental experiences. They will include you in their pain and passion, their joy and sorrow. They will not leave you in the cold, as it were, as you try to figure out where you belong. Instead, they will bring you in. They will include you as an insider, and they will love you no matter what.

E – a true friend will **ENCOURAGE** you. Gone are the days when haters can be called friends. If you can't rejoice for me then you don't deserve me. If you're always a voice of perpetual criticism and never a voice of constructive encouragement, then I want to know if you are my trainer or my friend. Trainers criticize. Friends encourage. As a friend, you should be a safe place where your friend can lay down. You should be a place of affirmation. You should be a constant reminder of their potential. They should be able to run to you with their dreams, goals, and ideas without you discouraging them! Friends encourage friends to be their best selves! Anything less than that, is a foe masquerading as a friend.

N – a true friend will **NEED** you. I've never met so many people who walk on eggshells before they ask for help. I've never met so many polite people who don't want to come off too needy or dependent. If I am your friend, I have no problem telling you when I need you. I need $20 until Friday. I need a shoulder to cry on. I need a ride to the supermarket. I need prayer before this pivotal meeting takes place. Prideful people don't need anybody. Their inability to confess a need reveals a heart too afraid to be human. But when you are truly friends with someone, you are unafraid to confess a need. And if your friend cannot meet that need, he or she is honest enough to tell you what they can do, instead of only telling you what they can't do. I don't know about you, but I need friends in my corner who will cheer me on.

I need friends who will show up at the hospital. I need friends who will hold me when my loved one passes. If there is no mutual need then there can be no reciprocal friendship.

D – a true friend **DESERVES** you and will **DECIDE** with you. A true friend will make your concerns their concerns. They will make your problems their problems; and when you have to make a decision, they will help you to think it through. They may not know the answer, but they won't leave you to figure it out alone. Be careful not to make crucial decisions with people who can't help you. Be careful not to get marriage advice from people who are happily single or terribly married. Be careful not to get financial advice from people drowning in debt. Obviously, anyone can tell you what you should do, but true friends have experience coupled with their advice. They don't just have head knowledge. They have life experience.

S – a friend will **STAND** by you. When people make mistakes, fans will run away from you. But friends will stand by you. Fans will distance themselves from you. But friends won't alienate you. You've got to learn how to stand with people because one day, you may need someone to stand with you. Don't turn on people because they made a bad choice. Life brings lessons so that we might learn how to be better people in the end. Your job is not to judge. Your job is to stand with. Friends don't need to know all of your business. They are just willing to be with you through the thick and the thin so that you don't have to go through this dark season alone.

POTENTIAL VERSUS PURPOSE

As you seek to place people in their rightful category, review this rubric in order to clearly see who people are in your life, not just who you want people to be. Most of us call people "friend" because we see their potential. But their reality is antithetical to what can be. We marry off of potential. We partner off of potential. But the wiser you become, the better your decisions will be. Perhaps you need to reclassify certain people after reading this chapter. Perhaps you need to re-evaluate the friendship because, after doing an assessment, you've realized that this is a one-sided relationship. In other words, you are doing more for them than they are doing for you. If that is the case, then make the necessary adjustments and do so with integrity and honor. Jesus didn't wait for us to love him back; He simply showed himself to be the true friend that he always was. In the same way, be who you are. Create boundaries when necessary, and ask God to bring people in your life who will not just tolerate you, but will also celebrate you.

CHAPTER 3

TYPES OF RELATIONSHIPS

When we talk about relationships today as a people with a 21st Century Westernized mindset, we imagine a reality about relationships (whether romantic or platonic) that didn't exist when the Bible was anthologized. In the Bible, for example, dating did not exist. Instead, the father would arrange the relationship, and the son didn't have much say in the selection of his bride. Marriages were arranged. The mother of the bride did not have much of a voice. Her role was to stay home and support the decisions of her husband. Thus, her interaction was just as minimal as the bride and groom. Yet, when we turn to scripture to look for people in the Bible who had marital problems, arguments between husbands and wives, and covenantal conflict, we find none in the Scripture. There were no major relationship challenges in marriages of old; and if marital challenges existed, they certainly were not recorded in Scripture.

In this chapter, I want to provide a practical framework on relationships so that you might have nuggets of wisdom to make better decisions. But I am setting the tone for this chapter in this manner because many people have rejected certain 21st Century ideas about dating, courting, friendship, and business partnerships under the excuse that something done or said in today's society, isn't biblical. I want to affirm unequivocally that this statement is true. Many things weren't discussed in the Bible because those issues didn't exist during Biblical days. So, if someone were to ask, "How does one date according to Scripture," I would tell them the truth. There is no biblical precedent or theological foundation for dating (as we have come to understand it) in the 66 books of the Bible. If someone were to ask how to vet or select a business partner according to Biblical recommendations, there is no verse in Scripture that you can turn to, which explicitly answers your questions in a literal way. Why? Because during biblical days, we didn't pick business partners like we pick them now. Either God told you to connect with someone, or your business partner was a family member who shared your last name or tribe. In the Bible, there was no such thing as "falling in love with each other" after a few dinner dates and movie nights. In Scripture, your dad was responsible for deciding. He made the decision without your input, and after you met one another, your marriage wasn't finalized until your covenant was consummated. If there was no blood on the sheets, then somebody was going to die! Imagine that? Imagine having no prior conversations with your lifelong partner? Imagine your father (yes, your dad) picking your future mate—as human and partial and overprotective as he is. When Abraham selected a wife for his son, Isaac, he sent a servant back to his hometown to select a wife. He trusted someone else to do the vetting, and when Rebekah arrived, she met her husband, Isaac, on the same day that their marriage was solidified. No marriage counseling. No fancy proposal. No Instagram pictures to post. Marriage was totally different back then. But does that mean we cannot turn to Scripture for wisdom about dating, friendship, and relationships? Absolutely not. The Scriptures were written for our edification, and the simple truths about platonic relationships also translate into romantic relationships. No matter where you find yourself on the relationship spectrum, allow this chapter to provide life principles on how to properly classify or quantify the relationships you currently have, and the relationships you aspire to have.

BAD COMPANY CORRUPTS GOOD CHARACTER

1 Corinthians 15:33 provides a very practical word of advice for all of us. Paul writes, "Don't be fooled by people who say such things, bad company corrupts good character" (New Living Translation). Any kind of company that can be categorized as bad, has the potential to corrupt you. Bad includes deceptive company, distracting company, diabolical company, competitive company, envious company, lustful company, idle company, procrastinatory company, negative company, pessimistic company, lazy company, wasteful company, seductive company, unstable company, unreliable company, greedy company—all of these areas have the potential to ruin your character. All of these categories can derail your focus and disrupt your progress. Why? Because the company your keep determines the quality of your life. The people who most speak to you, can alter

or reprogram the person that you are. We see this in our teenagers all of the time. If you train them to pay attention in school, they will start out one way. They will get dressed, go to school, do their homework, sit in the front of the classroom, schedule appointments for tutoring if they are struggling, and complete class assignments on time. But the moment they begin to congregate around students with other, ulterior motives, you see a shift in their zeal, excitement, drive, and participation. Their grades start to shift. Their outfits start to change. Their attitude of respectability, even in the home, becomes less honorable. Because the company you keep can empower you or deteriorate you.

You are the sum total of the people you hang around. If you were to tell me the 5 people you speak to and hang out with the most, I can tell you your future. I can predict how much money you make or will make. I can guess whether or not you own your home or live with your mom. I can tell if you've graduated from college or if you are in the military. I can tell if you are physically fit and disciplined. I can tell if you love your wife and children. I can tell a lot about you based on who you hang around. Because birds of a feather really do flock together.

Because we gravitate to environments that mirror our own priorities and desires. In the same way, our circle tells us about ourselves—and the moment God changes you, He often changes your circle at the same time.

This is why Proverbs 13:20 says, "Walk with the wise and become wise." Without question, wise people hang around wise things. Wise people have an appetite for knowledge and wisdom. Wise people are substantive. Wise people listen more than they speak. Wise people are not afraid to consult the source. Wise people are less impetuous than others. They are calculated and predictable. They take their time before making decisions. They don't live haphazardly through life without a plan. I highly doubt that you will ever hear a wise person say, "I will get up when I feel like getting up. If I get up after 2pm, so be it." Unless they are on vacation, wise people know the value of time and they wouldn't waste an entire day wallowing in the bed. Wise people make sacrifices. They understand that my body may be tired right now, but the reward of my resilience will pay off later. Wise people will not settle for the environment they find themselves in, if they are being challenged to grow, learn, and do more. Instead, they will search for opportunities to grow. Wise people understand that we grow based on what and who we are around. Unwise people don't think about that. But if you associate with fools, you will suffer harm. We need to explicitly have these hard conversations with our young people today. We need to tell them that if you are in the wrong car at the wrong time, you may end up getting charged for a crime you had nothing to do with. Why? Because when you associate with fools, you don't have to look for trouble—trouble will find you.

Who are you around? Who are the top 5 people you speak to or hang out with on a regular basis? When you are dating or getting to know someone, study their words but also pay attention to their friends. Find out who they talk to on a regular basis, and ask about their family life. If you pay attention in the beginning, you can safe guard yourself from being hurt in the end.

TRANSACTIONAL FRIENDS

The first category that you must understand in the categorization of all relationships, is a transactional friend. Transactional friends are only friends when we invite them into our lives to perform a certain task or deed. If a transaction is in progress, then they will be there.

Otherwise, they are not called upon for recreation or "down-time," they are here to perform a task or accomplish a goal. The guy who sold you a car? Transactional friendship. The woman who helped you with your taxes? Transactional friendship. The ex who only took you out to eat so that you weren't alone on Friday nights? Transactional friendship. These kinds of relationships are not intrinsically bad, but if you carry weighty expectations of these people, you will be disappointed. Learn to put people in their right category, and you will save yourself from lifelong pain and heartbreak.

CIRCLE OF FRIENDS

The next group is your circle of friends. Your "circle friends" are people who share the same circle, and for no other reason do we fellowship or interact. Circle friends work together. Circle friends attend the same church. Circle friends live in the same neighborhood, but if we are honest, we both know we wouldn't be friends without this common denominator. We are in close proximity with each other on a regular basis, so that is why we hang out and talk as much as we do. In this circle is where most friendships are ruined. Let me explain why.

Meet my friend Forrest. Forrest has a circle of other friends that I met when I met him. His other friends are Rob, Cliff and Jeff, and they are all his friends (not my friends). I just know Forrest. So, when I invited him over my house, he invited the friends whom he has always had a bond with before I met him. The problem is, Forrest and I have a bond that I don't have with the others in his circle. The connection between me and Rob, Cliff and Jeff is Forrest. Forrest is our bond. So if you start befriending Rob, Cliff and Jeff as if they are automatically your friend because you all share the same bond (Forrest) you will set yourself up for failure. Especially when Forrest does something wrong—you don't want to go to Rob, Cliff and Jeff about something Forrest did, because at the end of the day, they are ride-or-die for Forrest, not you. But when you don't properly assess who is in your circle, you will trespass on relationships that don't belong to you.

How many times have you ever been guilty of sharing something that you assumed was okay to share because all parties involved were in the same circle? I don't care how close of a circle it is, there's still a hierarchy in circles. Just because we're around each other doesn't mean we're equal in relationship. I may be in a circle of individuals but I value Forrest first, Rob second, and Cliff third. Though we're in the same circle, certain information is not public knowledge for everyone because trust is dispensed on a different level (even though we are in the same circle).

So, imagine: Forrest and I are good friends and ever since he's joined the team at my job, we've been bonding. But in the process of bonding with Forrest, I meet his friend Joel through Forrest. In the interim, Forrest tells me something that I think is okay to tell Joel. "Hey Joel. I was talking to Forrest the other day and he said he got evicted. Did he tell you that?" "No, he didn't. He'd never tell me that." Now you're stuck. You don't want Forrest to know that you have over-shared, and you don't want Joel to feel that he isn't as close to Forrest. How do we fix this? Most times, we make matters worse by telling Joel not to say anything to Forrest. This creates secrecy in their friendship and deception in yours. This is where we often mess up our relationships because Joel has never had allegiance to you. So of course, he will go back to Forrest with suspicion because it appears that you are sharing confidential information with people without permission. Don't be shocked when you are kicked out of circles, all because you didn't know how to manage certain relationships. Forrest's friends are not your friends! If you want to have good standing with Forrest, leave his circle alone until a natural, organic friendship is established over time with you and his crew.

COLLABORATIVE FRIENDS

Collaborative friends are the next category of relationships worth discussing. If you are my collaborative friend, then that means we are friends because we complement each other's weaknesses. As such, we support each other from that perspective. On a practical level, this might mean that we have to work together, but we don't have to like each other. We collaborate on projects because we both need to get the job done. Our departments cross-pollinate, and without their input, your job becomes more difficult. I call you my friend, but really you are my collaboration colleague. I know and you know that we can't get our goals accomplished unless we establish some level of communication and connection. But after the project is done, we are done. We aren't going out to eat. We aren't calling each other to check-in. Our relationship is business only. The more you mature, the more you will learn how to work with people you don't necessarily like. You will also learn how to collaborate with people you don't necessarily agree with. And if you want to go anywhere in the world, then you're going to have to learn how to make the best out of a bad situation. You won't always like everyone with whom you work, but you still need to get the job done.

Often times, the reason God won't elevate some of us is because we can't work with those who don't think like us. We have this kind of mentality: "If you don't think like me, then I will choose not to deal with you." And if we choose to live with that posture, then we will compromise our own success. Eventually, you will have to learn how to work with people who think totally different than you. You must learn to be diplomatic. It's about collaboration. It's about partnership. Not all partners will like each other but we do it because we all have a desired outcome—and by any means necessary, we've decided to put the purpose over our preferences.

PLATFORM FRIENDS

The next category is platform friendships. Platform friends are friends who give access to one another because one or both parties have a significant level of influence into a significant room that the other person needs to get inside of. Access is a privilege. Access should not be taken for granted; and Proverbs 25:7 says, "It's better to wait for an invitation to the head table than to be sent away in public disgrace." In other words, be humble when someone gives you access into a room you've never been in. Don't run for the head of the table. It's better to sit in the back and be invited to the front. When you have a platform friend, and God gives you access and influence to people in places you've never been to before, learn how to manage your promotion with confidentiality. Use discretion when posting about platforms you have just been introduced to. If God connects you to a high-profile client, don't boast. Let another man praise you. Telling everybody that you work with them, or giving out their number to people who don't know them, is only going to cause distrust. Just because you were given access doesn't mean you were given permission to share that access with everyone else. The quickest way to lose a platform friend is to post about it without permission. In all things relationship, be wise. I'm glad that the Lord has blessed you to know a lot of people. But keep that to yourself. I know that social media drives us toward likes and attention—but some things don't need to be posted in order to be proven. Keep some things a secret. Name-dropping is not attractive.

I'll never forget it. I was talking to a guy whom I thought was a really good guy...until he started bragging about who we knew and how he knew them. He came to look at a property for the church and he started out with, "Wow man, I was talking to _____ (a mutual friend of ours, whose name carries significant weight). Him mentioning this person had nothing to do with the matter at hand, so I dismissed it and kept moving. Then he went on to talk about how good a friend he was with this person. His over-emphasis on the relationship was almost excessive and idolatrous. Then he started giving out information that I know wasn't true. He said this person was working on a degree that he had already obtained, and before long, I figured out that this man was not as close to the man he had claimed to be friends with. I wouldn't be surprised if the esteemed individual didn't know him at all.

Platform people tend to blow up a relationship bigger than it needs to be. They exaggerate the extent of your relationship and in order to manage those relationships, you've got to be careful what you say around them. You must understand that people will tell you who they are in small words, and those small words are clues that expose who they really are in real life.

ASSOCIATE FRIENDS

Associate friends are only friends because they occupy the same position or have a similar experience in vocation or calling. Associate friends work together. Associate friends only deal with each other because they have a common cause or common mission. Outside of work, there's no real relationship. When I worked in the market place, I remember how every day, I'd see people talking in the cubicle. By the time they went to the break room, everybody was talking about what someone else said in the cubicle. They were only associates. They didn't care about one another. They were participating in gossip and they wanted to talk to each other to kill time. Associate friends pretend to be happy for you when you get promoted, but they will tear you down if they have an opportunity to take your job. If God favors you with a job where you have Saturday's off and everyone else is working on

Saturday, don't go around boasting to associate friends about how grateful you are that you don't have to work on Saturday's. Keep that between you and the boss. Why? Because if you keep on discussing it, people will take the information you provide, and twist it so that you have to work just like they have to work. There's no real loyalty in associate relationships, so don't look for loyalty in places that are only about accomplishing a goal. Remember: the same one congratulating you on your new position today, will be recommending your termination if your presence ever threatens their ability to be compensated.

TOLERATED FRIENDS

Tolerated friends are people you have to tolerate because losing their friendship will cost you other relationships that are more valuable to you. An example of a tolerated friend might be a mother-in-law or a stepfather. If you are honest, you don't like dealing with the person but you have to tolerate them because that person is connected to someone that you enjoy dealing with. Another example of a tolerated friendship is someone you have to manage wisely because they tend to be overly sensitive or extremely petty. These people occupy high power positions, so you know if you were to terminate the relationship, they would use it as an opportunity to destroy you. Petty people will shut down doors of opportunity for you when they see that you are moving on without them. Petty people will compromise your next level when they see you growing above their pay grade. So, in life you will have to tolerate certain people, but remember—you don't need to bring them closer to you out of guilt or fear. If someone wants to destroy your character, they will do so no matter how much you try to keep the peace. Your job is to maintain a healthy relationship with them so that they can't use anything you did or said, against you.

COVENANT FRIENDS

Covenant friends are the most expensive of them all. Covenant friends are valuable. Covenant friends are priceless. Most of us don't have more than two or three friends in this category, but knowing what to look for will help you not to incorrectly categorize someone in the wrong place. Covenant friends not only care about what you do; they also care about who you are. They couldn't care less how rich you are or poor you are. They love you for you. In life, covenant friends are rare. You don't meet many people who love you unconditionally; so, when you find someone who does, value them. Don't pour more into associates and platform friends than you do covenant friends. Don't water the areas of your life that you will reap the least amount of love from. Instead, water the areas of your life where you will glean the most from. Water your marriage. Water your siblings. Water your mother and father—after all, they brought you into the world, and they won't be around forever. Water your "Day 1 friends" who have seen you throughout the seasons, and still show up when you're having a bad day. Whatever you water, you will reap from. Whatever you invest in, will invest into you.

CHAPTER 4

WHEN FRIENDS BECOME FOES

If I were to take a survey, we all have an individual that we used to talk to, that we used to be in relationship with and for some odd reason, we don't talk anymore. There is probably somebody that you used to have fellowship with, used to go out with, but for some weird reason, the communication is almost nonexistent. Maybe you know what happened. But often times, we don't know what happened. I want to take a moment to talk about this particular subject. I want to begin by using two characters from Scripture that identify and personify this ideology very well. This gentleman used in this Matthian text is written to highlight some interesting things. Matthew 11 is upon the scene when Jesus is talking to His disciples and John, His good friend, his cousin, beloved, homeboy, ace, and bff. Luke 1:40-42 tells us that when Mary was pregnant with Jesus, Elizabeth was pregnant with John. When they came together belly to belly, their bellies started jumping because they recognized each other in the womb. They were cousins. They were kinfolk. I could imagine Mary who was six months behind Elizabeth, when Elizabeth had this child and named him John and Mary had her Child and named Him, Jesus, and indulge my personality for a moment, that they probably played cards together or had sleepovers where Jesus would come over to Elizabeth's house and John would go to Jesus' house and they would just have a good time. John and Jesus were going to the temple and learning the Word because obviously they knew the Word fluently. Not just that they knew the Word but that they also were just good buddies, playing ball together, playing softball together, telling on each other, just having good old times. They grow up and they're friends and they got a relationship together and John is out there preaching while Jesus is in the shadows. John is telling everybody, "Behold! The Lamb of God who comes into the world. There's a Man of God coming even better than me. I can't even loosen His sandals. He's not just my Cousin. He's also the

Messiah and my Friend. His name is Jesus." But all of a sudden John is preparing the way for Jesus, training his disciples, training his followers and then goes to them, "Listen, ya'll have been following me for a while. But I need you to stop following me and start following a guy named Jesus so He can lead you further than I could ever leave you. He's not just a Messiah to me. He's not just a Cousin. He's also my Friend." But all of a sudden John gets into a situation where he's in prison. Now he has a word to tell his Friend, Jesus. This is where we pick up in Matthew chapter 11. "When Jesus had finished giving His instructions to His 12 disciples, He went out to teach and preach in towns throughout the region. John the Baptist who was in prison heard about all these things and what the Messiah was doing. So he sent the disciples to ask Jesus, "Are you the Messiah we keep expecting or should we be looking for somebody else?" Jesus said, "Go back to John and tell him what you have heard and seen. The blind see. The lepers are cured. The deaf hear. The dead are raised to life and good news is being preached to the poor and tell him that God blesses those who do not turn away because of Me." Luke's gospel records, "Blessed are those who do not hear and do not see (yet believe)."

All of a sudden John gets incarcerated and starts raising questions about the guy he proclaimed was the One. Don't look at John with that type of attitude because many of us when we got into a situation that we didn't think was pleasant and we started asking the same questions. "Is He really the One or should we go look for somebody else. I don't think this Jesus thing is working out for me anymore because I find myself in a situation that I don't agree with and I think I need to look for somebody else." Many of us were like John too. But I want to talk from this idea as to how this tension might have come about. The text doesn't tell us how the tension had come about but we could suppose how this tension came about. How do two people who grew up as best friends now separate because of life's circumstances?

Number 1, if you're reading this text you'll probably find out that John let his feelings dictate the meaning of the relationship. It's very difficult to sit in prison, hear about Jesus healing other people and trying to figure out, "If He's healing people, He's opening people's eyes, if deaf people are hearing, how come He can't get me out of jail?" His heart is probably wondering, "Jesus is doing all of these great things, why in the world hasn't He come to get me?" You know how we do when people are talking about how God blessed them and we're sitting there wondering, "Well wait a minute. I've been praying to God too and obviously He listens because He answered your prayer and He ain't heard mine. I'm kind of tripping because how is it that God is responding to you and I've been calling Him all week and He ain't called me back?" So he's sitting there probably thinking this. And we've got to be careful that we don't let our feelings dictate the meaning of a relationship because your feelings will have you walking out of things that you need to stay in. Do you know your feelings can't be trusted? I remember one day I was at the gym and I was doing legs and I decided to run and play ball and I played so horrible and my feelings said, "Just give it up, you're getting old, people are running by you on the court, you just need to let it go." I was really disappointed in my performance and I had thought to myself," You know what? I really am just going to quit and maybe play here and there and not as serious as I normally try to play." But the next week I decided, "You know what? I'm not going to work on my legs but I'm going to go play ball one last time and see how I do. If I do good then I'm going to continue on."

Well it was the best performance I had all year and I'm so glad I didn't give my sneakers up too early because there's another Lebron James on that basketball court that I'm going to inspire to be great. What I'm saying is that your feelings could have you feeling a certain way that's not necessarily true. So you can't always go by your feelings because feelings change. They sway.

Number 2 is sometimes you gotta relocate to recalibrate. What I mean by that is when John was secluded away in a prison cell, not a prison cell like 33rd, but he had like rat feces all around him. They got people peeing beside him because there was no sanitary issues. So you gotta imagine the filth that he was in and how he feels. "Wait a minute. Why am I here? Why am I even in this? It stinks. It's terrible. There's no real sanitary walls. There's feces all around me. It's horrible. I can't even eat in this condition. Even if I wanted to eat I feel like I'm going to vomit because of the smell." But you've gotta be careful when you're by yourself because sometimes when you're by yourself, you'll make decisions that don't have all the facts. It's like going and stepping on the scale at Publix. You ever step on a scale at Publix and feel like you lost a lot of weight? Like, "Whoo, thank You Jesus!

Man I lost ten pounds!" Then you go to the doctor and he tells you that you're 15 pounds overweight and you're like, "Wait. I was at Publix and it said-" Right, because the scale was not calibrated right. You cannot make right decisions with wrong information. So while you sit isolated, for some of us that's why God said, "It's not good for man to be alone." It's not that being alone is bad. It's just that when you sit and you're alone too long, dangerous things start to happen. You know when you're alone that you talk yourself into things that people could have talked you out of. You motivate yourself to do things that you never would have done had you ran it by somebody else because being alone is not always a good thing. Be afraid of the person who likes to be by themselves because in the secrecy, that's where their sin lies. Be careful when you see people who like to be alone because being alone speaks to who you really are. You're not a reflection of what you do when people are looking. You're a reflection of what you do when people are not looking. So you gotta make sure you have the right thing.

Here's the other piece and this one is kind of unique. John must have been wrestling with Jesus' position and potential. Here it is his disciples (**John's**) are coming to him and telling him what Jesus told them. You gotta remember John taught them first. Jesus inherited their membership. Those were John's church member's first. So when John is hearing that Jesus is teaching them something, he's probably feeling some type of way because he was saying, "Wait a minute, I was your pastor first. Before you met Pastor Jesus I was your pastor. What do you mean Pastor Jesus told you this?! You tell Pastor Jesus, is He the One or shall we look for another?" Because it's hard for two people to share the same stage. That's why in marriage God gives us roles because He knows it's difficult for us to share the same platform. Look at it; whenever two people are in control, there's always chaos because it's difficult for two people to share the same platform. That's why you can't have two presidents. You have a president and a vice president. God doesn't give us titles because He is a title God, He gives us titles for clear distinction and function because if you don't know where you function, you'll start operating in my lane thinking that it's yours. But it's hard for you to decrease and let somebody else increase. It's like you're on your job talking to your boss and he says, "Man, you did a great job. But ever since we hired the new guy, he shows us how much better he is than you."

That's exactly what was happening. Jesus is the new guy on the block. Everyone is flocking to Jesus and everybody is talking. Let me pause and rewind for a second. I know when I said, 'When Friends Become Foes' you started thinking about all the people that stopped talking to you and all the people that are enemies towards you. But I don't want you to focus on just that side of the coin. I want you to flip to the other side of the coin and realize that you to have become an enemy of someone based on the way you acted. It's not always everybody else who's hating, sometimes you're somebody else's hater. Here's a quote from me, "When you're moment is maximized, they feel their relevance is minimized." So it means that when God opens a new door for you and someone used to be in the same platform as you, when they feel they are being minimized, they can't handle the maximization happening in your life. Let's say they're a singer and they sing every week. All of a sudden someone new comes up and everyone's like, "Oh that new singer is incredible," and the old singer goes, "They were alright, they weren't all that." Why? Because you don't like seeing other people maximize in your place because we gotta watch our heart. That's the other side of the coin. And sometimes as friends we're insensitive to the situations of our friends. So you know your friend just lost a child and here you are calling them and telling them, "Girl, I'm seven months pregnant." You think they're going to rejoice with you and they do but you're rejoicing and your celebration is causing them greater pain. So you gotta be wise in how you share what could be shared because not all blessings are meant to be revealed. It's not that they're against you, they're not in a position to handle it. If I'm catching the bus and I'm calling you and asking you, "Yo man, where you at?" "Oh, I'm catching bus 37, it's going to take me to such and such place before taking the transfer bus 25 to get to such and such." "Well man I just left the Mazerati dealership, I just bought a Mazerati." Wait a minute, this person is catching the bus and you're telling them about the car your about to drive? What I'm saying is they end up disliking you not because of you. But because they don't know how to say it with you being insensitive to the life that they're in currently. So we gotta be wise with how we showcase what God is doing in our lives compared to the person we're showcasing it to because it's very critical.

But not just that, John had an interesting time because comparison was the compromiser. The Bible says in Proverbs, "He that compares himself is unwise." Whenever you start comparing yourself to somebody else, you're bound to realize there's something lacking in what you have. If you start comparing yourself to other people who have more than you, you'll start being ungrateful for what you do have. If you start comparing yourself to the healthy relationship that they have, you'll begin to invalidate the security that you have in yours. When John started hearing people share their excitement of what Jesus was doing, compromise started happening because comparison began to be the case. You gotta be careful because people make us compete. You're on the job and you hear things like, "You do a good job but that other person can't touch what you do." Yeah you're right because life is all about competition. "How many people did you have at your wedding? I had 50." "Well I had 100." "How many karats was your ring? Mine was two." "Mine was four." "What kind of car do you drive? I have a Corolla." "Me too. What year is yours? Mine was 2002." "2004." Because we want to feel like we edged a person out because when you compare yourself, you're unwise. Why do you think the industry of plastic surgery happens to be doing so well? Because people are constantly comparing themselves and realizing and feeling that they are missing something. So they're like, "Pastor, if my butt was bigger I'd be happier. I'm going down to Miami so they can take the fat out of my legs and put it in my butt because I want to be able to-" When you compare yourself this happens.

Let me tell you how to handle your foes that we find in the text of Matthew 11 in the book. They come to Jesus and they say, "Jesus, are You the One or shall we look for another?" That may not mean much to you but people come to you with nonsense like, "Ay, you hear what such and such said about you? I wanted to tell you what such and such said," because they want your response. Let me give you a very important word. Silence can't be misquoted. There are some things that people bring you that you don't need to comment about. Some of you are getting disqualified for promotion because you think everything requires your comment. Silence cannot be misquoted. They're coming to Him like, "Yo Jesus, Your homie John? He's selling out. He throwing shade at You, Man. My cousin was by the prison the other day and I was stopping by to give him some commissary money and he just told me that he heard John say, "Are You the

One? Or shall we look for another?" Jesus recognizes that He has somebody that used to be blood of His blood and flesh of His flesh but has now dishonored Him. Jesus could have responded like Mercy Drive or Pine Hills on em and said, "Hold up. Nobody try me. Go get Me the sword, we gonna fix this." No, Jesus showed how to respond to people who are critical to us and He shows us how to do it with great dignity.

Number one, Jesus says, "Tell John, the blind see, the deaf hear and the lepers walk." Then He says, "Let Me further go on to talk about John. John was a good man and he preached to us and he led us. There's no greater man in history than John. Jesus does something very good; He speaks well of him **(John)** publically. You don't criticize your foes publically because if you criticize them, you feed them and whatever you feed, grows. If you starve them from getting attention, they won't grow. But if you feed them, they will grow. "Man I keep having war go on with my cousin." You know why? Because you keep feeding her. You keep going to your other cousin and telling her how you feel about the other cousin you don't like and the other cousin goes back and tells the other cousin and it keeps on growing because what you feed keeps on living.

Number two. Jesus only addresses him once. Nowhere in Jesus' ministry do you see Him continually mention John the Baptist. He doesn't go on about it. He just addresses it one time and keeps it moving because you've got to understand if somebody has an offence with you, Matthew 5, and you figure it out, you need to leave your gift at the altar and then go by them and then make it right with them. But after you have tried to make it right with them and they don't receive you keep on moving because after I've addressed you once, I don't need to address you twice. If I ask you for forgiveness and you refuse to extend the graciousness of forgiveness to me, then I have the right to move on and I don't have to continue to ask you for forgiveness. I tried to do everything I could to reconcile this relationship but you don't want to be reconciled so I am going to have to learn how to move on.

And when I move on, number 3 is, don't give them relevance through your position or your sphere of influence. Imagine if Jesus kept referencing John, His former disciples would be like, "Well if you keep talking with John, we may as well go back to John." But Jesus doesn't mention him because he doesn't deserve the attention now that you've moved on. If they're out of your life, stop looking at their page. They are no longer necessary. You're trying to see if they're happy. If they don't like you, move on. Cut them so far that they don't even know how to find you. That's not what Jesus would do? No, Jesus would forgive them but Jesus doesn't need them around. If you know that person is poisonous, there's no sense in sitting around their table. You know a lot of the trauma we're having is because we're going back to the snake and getting mad that it bites us. It's a snake, that's what it does. Let me put it in a different context. Don't give exposure to what deserves closure. You know why you keep getting hurt by him or her is because you keep opening the door that's been closed for a long time. "I wanna move on from her Pastor." But every time you say you wanna move on you keep looking at her profile. It's hard to close a door in which you keep playing with the knob. You gotta learn how to close the door.

Number four is an acronym for foe. F is for forgive them. Jesus didn't hold John in His heart. He let John be. John's going to do his thing, I forgive him. Forgiveness is not forgetting but releasing. What marriage really is in short, marriage is the collection of two great forgivers. Think about it. Because if you cannot forgive, you cannot love. Your marriage and relationships stop moving forward at the moment you stop forgiving. So if you cannot forgive, you've just inhibited yourself to love. The reason why Jesus' love is always eternal for us because it's always forgiving. So you gotta learn how to forgive. We have to learn how to be master forgivers. Now if you grow in life, you will be hurt in life. But you still gotta learn how to forgive. Some of us are so broken from what people have done that we can't receive new people because of the hurts of old people. But you've gotta learn how to still operate with pain in your heart because it will not stop you from being hurt again. You putting up the walls that you have thinking they are self-preservation mechanisms, they don't help you all the time, they hurt you because God is trying to send people to help you but because of your walls they can't get in because you are hidden and trying to protect yourself from the pain that somebody else did to you yesterday. The struggle with that is that you're allowing someone to live in your life that should be out of your life and they're living through your life and closing opportunities to you because you have given them the key to your future. Forgiveness is about releasing because if I release you then it no longer holds me captive. When you don't forgive it causes side effects; bitterness, anger, discontention. All of these things in your heart. I don't care if someone stole $10,000, $100,000, $50,000 from you. You gotta learn how to just say, "You know what? I'll never loan them money again but I forgive them." This next point is very critical because if you don't follow it, you're in trouble. Observe your heart so you don't become what you despise. I was in Dallas for two days at a session and this successful 32 year old from one of the largest financers from private wealth. He dealt with wealth management of millionaires. He's married, got kids and he began to share his stories of how he travelled up the ladder of success. He shared how his father was so horrible, he would have been better in a single parent household because his dad was abusive, a drunk, and didn't do very good by his mother. So three weeks before he decided to go visit his dad who was dying of cancer. He said that it took a lot for him to even be at his bedside because he just hated him that much. He said that his father looked up at him and said, "Son, I know you're not happy with me but I did my best to raise you. I just didn't treat your mother well but I did the best that I could. But son, what I need to tell you is that you need to get over it and forgive me." He said, "At that moment I wanted to tell my father that he had no right to ask me to forgive him because you weren't there and you treated my mother horribly. You treated my siblings bad. I wanted to go off on him. But something told me to hold my peace." His father leaned in and said, "Because if you don't forgive me, you'll become what you dislike." So the man began to cry because it was that moment where he realized that moment was key to becoming someone who he didn't want to become. It was by observing your heart not to become what you despise. I want to park there because E stands for execute your purpose which is how Jesus decided to handle John. "If he's not going to believe in Me, I'm not going to get in a fight or argue with John. I'm not going to talk about John's mama. I'm just going to tell John, "The blind see. The deaf hear..." So in essence what He's saying is, I'll let my purpose do my communicating, as opposed into getting into a tit for tat match. It's important to let the vision and works that God says to do, do the talking. God says at that point the vision will speak. Basically God is saying, let your vision do the talking and don't worry about addressing your critics because they will always be there. They will always be there. You will never please everybody. So that's why you have to live according to your own convictions.

I want to stop at number five. Observe your heart so you don't become what you despise. Some of you have strong hatred towards somebody. You just strongly hate them. And you might be absolutely right that everything they did was horrible. Everything they did was wrong. But like the father said, "If you don't forgive you'll become what you despise. You gotta learn to let people go. Some of us have people on our hearts and we've had them on our hearts for years. Jesus tries to make it even tough on you to say, "If you want to pray, leave your gift and go make it right because He knows the importance of being able to release people. The power of Jesus did not stop the hurt from the person of Jesus. Jesus still experienced pain, hurt and aggravation. But He still had an obligation to let people go. That doesn't mean I forgot but it means I released you. I know I released you because when I see you, I don't feel the same way I felt when you offended me. If you put all the effort into executing your vision as you did with holding people in your heart, you could go so much further.

I'll close with this story. I remember my dad had a weird, unique upbringing. He raised himself practically. My father's father died when he was twelve. So his ability to be a father came from him just guessing. There was no manual or rulebook to be a good dad or a good parent. As much of us that think we're a good parent, there's no book out there that says this is how you be a good parent because it's subject from child to child. Each child is different. What works with one child does not work with the other child. It's not one size fits all. So everybody in our family ended up pretty much hating this guy because he was a strict, militant guy. His yes was yes. His no was no. There was no having fun around him, he was just a very stern individual. I remember and I think it was my 18th birthday, I come home and this guy always looks for reasons to fight with you. So I get home and his car is there and I'm like, "Oh Lord, God help us." You know it's bad when you see your parent's car and you're like, "Oh shoot, here we go." I go inside and as I open the door I'm like, "Hi dad, how are you?"

He's like, "Good and you?" He asked about school and I was like, "Good." He found something so little to argue about so much so he would be like, "Pack up all your stuff and get out." This is on my birthday. So I'm gathering my stuff, I'm getting out. I remember I had a little, blue Toyota Corolla with 17s on there, two 10s and a trunk. (?) I'm taking my stuff and I'm getting out. I remember just saying, "Man, I so hate you." And he looked at me and said, "You're not the first." I grab my stuff thinking, I hate this guy. This guy's such a jerk. It comes about earlier in my life that my dad was rough. I remember my dad was telling me that my sister was dating this crazy guy and all her boyfriends were typically crazy and he said was related to Richard Prior. I was like dad, "This guy's a con artist." He was like, "No he's not. He's my son." I was like, "I think you think he's your son because he's rich." So long story short, what this guy would do to make money is that he would take checks and make counterfeit checks. And so he was able to pretend he had money because he was writing counterfeit checks. My dad would look at me and say, "You talk about my son one more time, I'm going to pray to God that you sell nothing but newspaper the rest of your life." You know at that moment I felt like I just wanted to strangle him and that it would be okay. But several years down the line I heard my dad say something that just completely changed my mind in this concept on forgiveness. My dad goes, "My children don't love me." And he wasn't talking to me, he was just talking. He said, "My children don't love me, but they didn't know that I didn't know how to be a father. I had to raise my brother and sisters at 12 years old. They think I don't love them but it's just that I really don't know what love is." So that moment just liberated my thought. That a man was only doing his best in the way he knew how because his definition of love was let me provide for you because my provision died. So his interpretation of love was, if I give you provision, that is what love is. So sometimes we hold people hostage for an ability that they don't have to give. Most of you are holding people hostage and they were giving you their best. Until you learn how to release people, you'll never prosper. My father comes here every week. I call him an enjoyable, old man. He has his ways but he's an enjoyable old man. But my life never prospered until I learned to recognize that I needed to learn how to forgive. Or like the father said, "If you don't forgive, you will become what you don't like." So I'm encouraging you to go deep in that soul of yours and pull from the well of forgiveness. You now typically if you hate your mother or father, I pray to God that your seed doesn't reciprocate that to you because life has a funny way of giving us harvest that we don't want.

MENTORSHIP & MILLENNIALS

I used to work for Zachary Tims at New Destiny Christian Center with my good friend, Andre. Andre was bigger than life, and I mean that literally. He had this little Chevy and I'd laugh when he'd pull up to places. He'd get out of the car knowing full well what I was laughing at and he'd always say, "you know this is all I can afford!"

That is until he got fired. We were making $25,000 a year at NDCC filing papers. At 21 years old, with a college degree, we filed documents and bills, documents and bills, documents...and bills... The filing department knows everything: how much that building costs to build, how expensive it is to keep the lights on, those billboards on the highway and how the ones that stand out the most come with the biggest price tag, how many church members it takes to hire the landscapers every month, etc. Andre and I went into ministry all fired up to change the world, heal the sick, give sight to the blind, walk on water, and here we were stuffing envelopes and sitting on ice packs at the end of the day because those chairs wore out their comfort level. I was almost jealous when Andre got let go, but it wasn't long until he came to me with some news.

"This church down the street wants to pay me $50,000 as a youth pastor," he said. Have you ever simultaneously felt joy and depression? It's like when someone kicks you in the gut and you fall into a flower bed, those daffodils smell like heaven but that ache in your stomach might lead to internal bleeding. It's the feeling you get when a good friend tells you he is making double than what you're making, when the week before he was making the same as you.

A few weeks and a legion of filing drawers opening and closing later, I get a call, "you can make $40,000. Come be our young adult leader." Those daffodils smelled so much sweeter now. Me, a 21-year-old, making $40,000? That's a lot of cash, and I already knew what I was going to do with all that money. All I had to do was go to my pastor and tell him, *hey I got a better job offer what are you going to do about it?*

You feel good when you get another job. You square up your shoulders, you feel strong, you can chew nails. I knocked on Pastor Zach's office and he offered me to sit down. Andre is big, yeah, but Pastor Zach was a giant. His presence filled the entire office that day. My shoulders went oval shape, and those nails I was chewing, turned into marbles.

"What's on your mind," he said. His voice thundered even though he was almost whispering.

"Yeah," I said. "I got another job that's going to pay me more and they're going to pay me $40,000 to be their young adult leader. I just want to know what you're going to do." This man, I promise you not, turned his chair so all I was looking at was the back of his head. Those few seconds of silence, hurt. If I shifted my weight, the chair squeaked. I swear I could hear the clicking of his Rolex hit the desk, and the tapping of his fingers while his hands were in a prayer shape.

"Go," he said. "Take the money. But if you do, then you will never see greatness." He was talking directly at the back of the wall, but it felt like his lips were centimeters from my ear. I wanted the money, but I wanted recognition, too. How could it be so easy just to let me go?

"They are offering me more money because they see my value," I said.

"I said you can go. Take the money. What I'm giving you is far greater than money can ever buy." He turned his chair around and looked straight into me. "Most people don't realize it until they lose it."

THE PRICE OF MENTORSHIP: IT'S ABOUT THE PROCESS

Elijah said to Elisha, "Ask what I shall do for you before I am taken from you." Elisha said, "Please, let a double portion of your spirit be upon me."

–2 Kings 2:9

We want what we see but we don't understand the price, the process, and the plan. You can be told the price, the process, and the plan, but all you are seeing is what you want. There's a difference between knowing how to get there and experiencing how to get there.

Elijah was a great prophet and mentored Elisha, who was a lowly farmer. They may have had similar names, but there was no relation, and they were very different men. Elijah was a private person. He kept things short and never said much, so when he did say something…everyone paid attention. Elisha was very talkative, hung out with everybody. He would stay at your home if you asked him. He also wanted to learn everything he could from Elijah, the man who spoke to three generations of kings. Elijah is who Elisha wanted to be. He said to Elisha, "if you follow me and make it out to the end, then I will give you what I have."

A lot of us who are in the church and/or the business world, want the mantle and the success. We want the promises. How often do we want the process? The mantle could mean success, the promises could bring wealth, but the process doesn't give you any of that. You suffer in the process, you get cut in the process. If you understand how the process works, then money will come eventually, but if you are in the dark you aren't looking for your glasses so you can see better. You need to turn on the lights. Some of us are so caught up in looking for the money that we let the experience pass us by. The value of money ebbs and flows, inflates and deflates. The value of experience, the evidence by which monetary gain is accumulated, that is priceless.

Elijah couldn't just give Elisha his spirit. What responsible prophet dishes out his blessings? This man of God needed to know that Elisha was the real deal. He needed to test Elisha's own spirit to see if he was capable of doing what is required of a prophet of the Most High. He had to know that Elisha loved him, not just what he had.

Just before God took Elijah to heaven in a whirlwind, Elijah and Elisha were on their way to Gilgal. Elijah said to Elisha, "stay here; the LORD has sent me to Bethel." But Elisha said, "as surely as the LORD lives and you live, I will not leave you." So they went down to Bethel.

–2 Kings 2:1-2

If you want what someone has, and you love them, then you will follow them where they go, and you will receive what they have. It doesn't matter where they are going, you go where they go because what is in them is greater than what's on television. You will absorb more information and more impartation by being around them than being away from them. If Elijah is going to Ocala, Elisha is going to be in Ocala. If Elijah is going to Tampa, Elisha is going to Tampa. Elisha heard Elijah is doing a Youtube video, he's going to watch that video. If Elijah is doing a Facebook Live, then Elisha is going to watch that stream and comment so his mentor knows he's there. If Elijah is going to do a Periscope, then Elisha is going to be on Periscope because whatever Elijah has Elisha wants in his life.

There's a difference between those who want it and those who think they want it. The proof of desire is pursuit. If you don't pursue, there's no proof that you have desire. If you desire it, you follow after it. Elisha is saying *wherever you go I'm going*. We see he has the desire because he has the pursuit.

The guild of prophets at Bethel come out to Elisha and ask, "Do you know that the Lord is going to take your master from you today?" Elisha says, "yes I know; now be quiet." Elijah tells Elisha he's going to Jericho, *stay here*. Now Elisha has an opportunity to rest. He has every excuse to take a break, relax with the prophets at Bethel. His master even said to stay. He's giving him a break. Bethel is *the House of Bread*. It's the place where you're fed. Where God speaks to you. It's where you come and eat from the Master's Table. It's where God sustains you, an easy place because when you go to Bethel, you begin to start thinking that God is letting you go to rest it out.

The thing about God, though, is that he moves to shake things up just when it looks like it's going to be easy. He won't leave you in one place. He will take you to different places even though you're comfortable and not ready to go because he has a plan for you. And so Elisha says, "As surely as the LORD lives and you live, I will not leave you." The pursuit fuels the desire.

The same thing happens in Jericho. The guild of prophets here ask Elisha if he knows the Lord is going to take his master, his mentor, away. Elisha says, "yes I know; now be quiet." Elisha knows what his master is doing, where his master is going, because he is experiencing everything along with him. So when Elijah gives Elisha a break again, telling him to stay here in Jericho so Elijah can go to Jordan, again Elisha says, "As surely as the LORD lives and you live, I will not leave you."

Finally on their way to Jordan, fifty men from the company of prophets stood at a distance, facing the place where Elijah and Elisha had stopped at the Jordan River. Elijah took his cloak, rolled it up, and struck the water. The water divided to the right and to the left, and the two of them crossed over dry ground. Notice what he did, or more so what he didn't do: there was no step one, step two, step three, Elijah didn't teach Elisha how to part the river, he just did it, and Elisha observed. He experienced how to overcome an obstacle and nothing was said between them.

After they crossed the river is when Elijah asked Elisha what he could do for his apprentice before he was taken away. Elisha asks for the double portion of his mentor's spirit. You might say *how bold it is to ask this*. But remember, Elijah is the type of person who only speaks when he needs to. He has purpose in his rhetoric. So when he asks a question, of what he can do for you, you better not take this opportunity for granted, but rather take advantage of this process. A double portion. Of course, Elijah remarks how difficult this is, but he never says it cannot be done. He says, "If you see me when I am taken from you, it will be yours—otherwise, it will not." Only if you are watching. Some of us are watching too many things at once when we should be watching the main thing. Where I move, you move. Follow your main thing. So when Elijah is taken up, by chariots of fire from heaven, a quantifiable miracle before Elisha's eyes, he is not overwhelmed by the sudden act of what is happening, but by the fate of his mentor, his teacher, his prophet. Elisha says, "Father! My Father!" He's not concerned about the mantle, the success, or the double portion, at that moment. He's concerned about the man. We often are more concerned about the mantle, or the anointing. But if you get the man, you get the mantle. Elisha went through many trials before he got that double anointing, because anything God has promised you, He will make sure you go through the process. God leads you to the anointing, so that you may endure until the end.

The race is not given to the swift nor the strong but he who endures until the end.

–Ecclesiastes 9:11

Once you've run your race, and you're still standing, now you have a reason to say, "the Lord has blessed me!" You never have to apologize for how you got to where you did because you went through the process, you weathered the storms. The race isn't about the fastest, it's not about who goes off first, but it's about who will finish the race at all.

A great mentor will always take you places. Even when you think they aren't taking you anywhere, you are going somewhere. Your mind will be stretched like a rubber band, and when it snaps back, you'll be sharper than before. No one can make you think bigger if you are happy thinking small. You will be challenged, and you'll feel like you don't know anything, but it's at that moment when you empty yourself, that you can be filled with who you were meant to be, a reached potential. There are Elisha's that think they are Elijah's. Elijah is trying to teach something, and those Elisha's think they know it all already, or that they know better, or maybe if Elijah could just write out a three-step-program then Elisha can figure it out on his own. You need to humble yourself and listen to somebody who has already been there, who can tell you how to get there, or else life will be a constant reflection of your own decisions

CUTTING THE FLESH FOR THE SPIRIT TO GROW

I stayed at NDCC. Not because I was offered more money to stay, but I realized what Pastor Zach was trying to tell me. Yes, I filed documents, and sorted bills, but in that paper work was the lifeblood in how a church is run and managed. I knew what land was good to build on, what kind of marketing strategy would be effective to reach the community, reasonable prices for maintenance, lessons that could only be taught through experience, the kind of lessons they don't go over in seminary. Some of us, like me, curse our promised land because we don't understand that God is training you so that you can do something great, but you don't see that. All you see is the mantle.

Pastor Zach had a Mercedes, and he would hand me the keys and tell me, "Go drive my car. Fill it up with gas." The joys of riding a Mercedes are unparalleled, especially when it isn't your own. There was one day when he said to take it home. I got to leave my beat up Corolla at work and drive that Mercedes into my driveway. I sat in the living room all night looking out the window, pretending that car was my own. I'd say *looks like I finally made it now.* I cherish that time. He was training me to think differently. He was forcing me to think like the man I would become. So then I decided to take every opportunity to be that man I was supposed to be, how Pastor Zach saw me.

I never let him pay for anything when I was around him. He needed windshield wipers for that Mercedes, and gave me $50 to pick them up. I refused his money. I went myself to Mercedes, pulled out a $20 and said, "let me get the windshield wipers for the S550." Well, they laughed and said to me that the price was $92, $72 of which I did not have. I charged the wipers on my card and returned after the errand was done.

"How much did it end up costing you," he asked me.

"Don't worry about," I said. "I've got you covered. I looked for every opportunity to serve, to sow with my finances. This little change in my thinking did something special. Someone would come up to me and say, "the Lord put you on my heart. I'm going to give you a seed." They would give me the very amount that I put out in order to serve my mentor. God was still on my side. I wanted to buy a home in my dream neighborhood, and the person selling me the house told me, "tell me what you can afford because I want you to have this house." What you sow today you will reap tomorrow.

It's not all fun and games and driving a Mercedes being the protégé. We'd go to the airport, and I'd have my suitcase as well as Pastor Zach's, and he'd be walking and have nothing in his hands. People told me how stupid I looked, letting this person take advantage of me. They didn't understand. Sometimes you need to lose in the moment in order to win in the long term. Humble yourself before man. The race was still underway.

Some time had passed, I'd become a newlywed, received a raise (making $40,000 now), but my friend was making a little more than I was. His church was not too far away, and he was doing what I was doing. I felt the sting again: my potential, my worth, my pride.

"You should be smart enough to make more money," he said to me.

So I'm sitting there thinking, how am I going to just make more money? Well, I went and received my real estate license. I started in 2006, and twelve years later I'm still in the business; good business. I noticed the church needed a lot of graphic design work, so I started my own graphic design company with a friend of mine. The church kept my design company busy, and we did well. I went up to Pastor Zach and said, "Sir, thank you for paying me more money."

"When did I pay you more money?" he said.

"That graphic design company that has been making your logos and building schematics for events: that's my company."

"You've been making me pay you? You finally got it. I didn't pay you more because it would cripple your creativity."

Most people don't want to be part of the process,
they just want to be a part of the outcome.

There should be no fat on any grilled steak. Period.

There should be no fat layer or fat chunks on a grilled steak, whether or not it is USDA Prime Grade. Any untrimmed fat layer and chunks will burn and taste horrible, and it will harm the taste of the entire steak.

Cut the fat.

Gilgal was the first stop for Elijah and Elisha, before Bethel, before *the House of Bread.* Gilgal was an interesting place; it was a weird place. This was the place of cutting, where the people would see the servants coming and say, "here we need to circumcise these grown men because they have some flesh that they can't take with them to Bethel." There were some areas that they had grown accustomed to that just didn't work in Gilgal. They had developed habits and they were not conducive enough to go to the next level. So they had to be cut, and it hurt.

God needs to grill you. He wants the best steak, better than USDA Prime Grade. You've got some fat around the edges though. If he keeps the fat there, then it's going to burn, and if you burn then you are ruined.

To keep you from burning, he needs to trim, he needs to cut you, and separate you from the others. But God doesn't cut you, he lets you do the cutting. He leaves it to you to trim your fat, to get rid of what's holding you back from your worth, your potential. We need to ask God to humble us before He humbles us Himself, and you don't want God cutting you.

He will lead you to Gilgal before he brings you to Bethel, so you can cut yourself, because the flesh you are carrying with you can contaminate where He's trying to take you. Gilgal is a tough place within the process. You'll walk around leaving hurt, with a limp. If it doesn't cost you anything, though, you won't appreciate eating the bread from the Master's Table. Now that's the interesting part. If you let yourself be cut down, will you continue to *the House of Bread?* Even though He has given you cause to bleed, will you still sit with Him? Will you trust Him, even though He's harmed you? When He tells you things you don't like, will you still listen? When your ego gets smashed, when your pride gets checked, and you walk away, well then you never sought for that mantle, that anointing in the first place.

We all enjoy when people tell us what we want to hear, when our ego is inflated. Mentors do not do that.

They are not in the business of inflation. Their currency never goes out of style. They can't give you anything if you've never went through anything. A mentor will make sure that when you are in Gilgal, all of your flesh is sliced clean off. God won't just cut you and leave you bleeding though. He will surgically repair you, and then feed you.

Don't let anyone cut you that doesn't have the power to heal you. When Elijah tells you to stay, what will your response be? Will you listen and stay, and watch and learn from afar? Or will you tell him, "where you go I will follow." If you are Elisha, then you know that you've been through too much to stop following. You gave up your comfortable life as a farmer, you learned how to sow seed and reap harvests. Perhaps you think your job is insignificant to your purpose, when all the while it's been a part of your purpose and your process, all along. When Elisha was a farmer, God was teaching him. He taught him that there will be seasons of plenty, seasons of dryness, and all of these seasons will be a part of his destiny. God will use that job that you think is purposeless, the job that has no future, God will use it to shape you, mold you. You need to keep moving, stop staying in one place. He wants you to go to Jericho.

Jericho is a crazy place. The church wants to shout about it, "I marched at the wall seven times!" That wasn't what made the walls come down, though. Jericho was a place of obedience to where you could obey God at what seemed like asinine instructions: march around the wall seven times and on the seventh step I want you to give Me praise. Now that makes no sense. Since when does praise knock down walls, God? And God says, "I don't want you to think about it and that's why I cut you." When God cuts you, you don't give Him a checklist why it's not a good idea. There are people around you that will tell you to stop pursuing because they won't see what you see; that's why you can't check with everybody about everything all of the time. That's why you can't ask everybody to tell you what they think because they aren't qualified to tell you what they think. The prophets told Elisha that his master was going to leave him, and he said to be quiet because he had to stay focused. The Jordan is Elisha's victory. He saw his master split the sea. And so when it came time, after the whirlwind took Elijah, for Elisha to split the seas, he did as he saw his master. He took his cloak, struck the sea, and the waters departed right to left. It is harder for a rich man to enter the Kingdom of

Heaven than it is for a camel to get through the eye of a needle. You can't reach your next level until you are low enough. You can't walk through that door because you are walking too tall. You've got to get low because what God is trying to do is humble you so you can remain teachable. When He can teach us, He can grow us. When Elijah went to the Jordan, he learned how to overcome the obstacle blocking his path.

In my real estate business, we were listing a property and it was a good property that many people would be interested in. I had my reservations, though. If I put my name out there with a sign that said *Call David Jacques for this property*, people who didn't even want the property would constantly barrage my phone. A gentleman was talking to me about this property and he proposed a deal after hearing me out: "I'll put my name on the property, just give me 5% of the deal." Now he's not making that much on the deal, but the experience of dealing with all of these phone calls, the people that are interested and not interested in the listing, the prank calls will give him something more than what 100% of the deal could give him. Here's the point: if you want to be mentored, then sometimes you need to take less in order to gain more.

CHAPTER 6

CIRCLES OF INFLUENCE

Circles are magnificent shapes. Big circles, small circles, microscopic circles, cosmic circles. Red circles, blue circles, green circles, magenta circles. Circles within circles. You can draw a square free hand, no problem; though, try and make a circle free hand and for some reason you'll almost always get an oval, which is just a stretched out circle, but it's not a *circle* circle.

Let's try and make a circle. You're going to need to find some tools. Unless you have a drafting compass handy, head over to Staples and ask the nice person with the red apron where you can find one. Make sure it is a *drafting* compass and not a *directional* compass (I'm unsure if they sell directional compasses at Staples, but I'd rather you not spend more money than you have to on account of me). If you use the wrong tools you will make the wrong shape. Now that you've got your compass, grab a pencil and paper. Put your pencil in the open leg of the compass. Adjust the compass for the radius of your circle; for a bigger circle, spread the compass wider. Set the stationary leg (the one with the sharp tip at the end) where you want the middle of the circle. Make contact with the pencil and paper and keep the stationary leg stable as you move the pencil leg around in a circle. Once you've collided the graphite with your starting point: congratulations! With the right tool, you've managed to create a perfect circle.

Here's another way you can make a circle. Grab that pencil you used for the compass, and get a new sheet of paper. Place the paper on a flat, clean surface. The easier the surface is to move on paper, the better, such as a well-polished table. Also, make sure you have plenty of space to move around. Place the pencil on the paper. Press down on the point where the exposed wood on the pencil meets the painted part. Have the tip of the pencil touch the paper, so that the eraser end is sticking up. While your index finger is holding the edge of the pencil, rotate the paper beneath the pencil with your free hand. Continue the rotation until a full circle is formed. How about that, another perfect circle! All you had to do was keep steady and change the environment around your target.

Here's the last one you can try. This time you're going to need a ruler, that same pencil, and another piece of paper. Draw a square. Divide the square equally into four smaller squares with the pencil and a ruler. Draw round lines in one smaller square by starting from one end of a bisecting line (the line that divided the square) and take the half circle shape up to the next bisecting line, with the rounded edge sitting against the edge of the large outer square. Repeat for each small square until one large circle has been created inside the large square. Wait, you're not done yet, you need to flip the pencil over and use the eraser on the square lines to leave behind the circle. At last, another perfect circle. All you needed to do was produce something you were never meaning to do in order to accomplish what you first set out to do.

Now get yourself one more sheet of paper and sharpen your pencil. Close your eyes and think about how a circle looks. You might be thinking about how the Earth looks in space, the top down view of a water bottle cap, the home button on an old iPhone. Okay, you got it? When you are ready, open your eyes and capture that shape onto the paper by making touchdown with the tip of the pencil and gesticulate your hand in a swirling motion.

Doesn't look much like a circle, does it? You're close, so very close to what you pictured, but something is just a little off…

Try it again. Think of the shape, swirl your hand on the paper—not much difference, huh? Actually I think the one you did just before looked better. Keep doing this until the page is black, or your pencil breaks (either through excessive use or the result of sheer frustration and an explosion of anger).

You may know exactly how a circle looks, the precise way how to make a circle, but unless you follow clear instructions and use the correct tools, you will almost never achieve the perfect free hand circle. Making perfect circles can be complicated; or you can exert more energy than you need to; or it can be as easy as fitting your priorities in the proper place and the shape virtually draws itself.

THE THREE CS: THE CROWD, THE CREW, AND THE CORE

Everyone that knows you doesn't know you, they know a piece of you. When you have the unfortunate circumstance to attend a funeral, you attempt to find comfort in the way the deceased's friends talk about him. I knew him as this, I know him as that. Together they combine the *pieces* of which they knew about him and put him together again. But unless you *knew* him, you'd never know if those pieces were really him, if they really represented his heart, who he truly was. Be careful when you are alive to prevent anyone from boxing you in, the only box people should put you in is the one you end up in when you die.

To recalibrate your relational IQ, you need to analyze your relationships, the people you are friends with, the people you love, and create circles for them, like boundaries. Often times we meet new people and they end up walking away not only knowing what we do for a living but what we had for breakfast, who we went to prom with, how fast we were going in the residential area on the way to church because we can't be late again for *another* Sunday. I call these people gushers. We gush! About our lives, our kid's lives, our mom's lives, we just spill everything out. Every now and then you need to stop and think to yourself, *did I just share the wrong piece of myself?* In order to not get hurt, though you will still get hurt, it is best to know how to classify people we have relation with. When you classify them correctly, you know the pieces you can share and the pieces you probably should never share.

Silence cannot be misquoted. People may come to you with information, perhaps something you said because you gave the wrong people the wrong piece of you, and you caused your brother to stumble. We can gossip by accident, it doesn't have to happen on purpose, just ask my mother. If you try and remember, though: silence cannot be misquoted, then gossip might as well be a spider on a wedding cake—it doesn't belong.

We classify relationships, the people around us, in an ever shrinking circle of trust. Our eyes, in order to function, are made up of a distinctive mechanism. The deeper you go, the more complicated the mechanism. The cornea is the transparent front part of the eye, and it contributes to most of the eye's focusing power, but its focus is fixed. Inside that is the iris. This is the color of the eye, and it controls how much light reaches the retina. Inside the iris is the pupil, the dark, black part of the eye. This is the eye's aperture, and it absorbs whatever light the iris brings in. When you are pleased by what you are seeing, your pupil expands, the blackness absorbs almost most of the eye. Have your significant other take a look at you and gaze into their eyes, look directly into their pupil. You'll get to see how attractive you are to that person. All of these layers are critical in how we see the world. The way we see our relationships are just as complex.

These are the three layers you need to recalibrate your relationships so you can see clearly the people in your circle of influence: The Crowd, The Crew, and The Core.

Draw a circle again, use one of the strategies we talked about earlier. This time make it a big circle, make it fit the whole page. This is The Crowd, your largest circle of influence. These are the people you meet in your day to day, the people you sit behind in church, the people at your job. The Crowd is a group of people you end up gathering with. They know who you are and they know about you, they know what you do. You catch up every now and then when you are aren't busy and you happen to run into them. It's the: *he's that guy who did that thing one time.*

Make another circle inside this circle, so that means it's going to be smaller, a lesser radius, a few notches in on the leg of the drafting compass. This is The Crew. These are the people you talk to on a regular basis. You stay in the lobby after church and you have to say hello and see how their week went. You invite them over for barbecues. They know a lot of what's in your head, but only The Core knows what's in your heart.

Last circle, I promise. This one is inside the circle you made before—this is called The Core. This is the smallest circle of influence. These individuals carry the charisma, the character, and the chemistry to know and understand the things of your heart. These are the friends that don't take sides because circles don't have sides! They stand by the truth, the kind of truth that sets you free.

> *...many in the crowd believed in him, They said, "When the Messiah comes, will he perform more signs than this man?"*
>
> –John 7:31

Jesus had his own circles of influence. He had many circles of influence: The Multitude, The Seventy, The Twelve, The Three, The One. The Crowd saw Jesus do miracles. The Crowd was The Multitude, The 5000, but they didn't see him when he was tired, when he cried tears of blood, when he prayed that hopeful prayer for the cup to pass from Him, lest the will of the Father be done. The Crowd also said that Jesus was demon-possessed—they were also the ones shouting for Barabbas to be spared, and for Jesus to die a traitor's death.

The Lord had The Crew, The Twelve Disciples. They professed His rightful place as the son of man. They performed miracles and baptized in His name. They broke bread together, drank wine together. Even when the seas met with stormy gales, they trusted in Jesus to calm the waters and still the winds. But they also betrayed Him, one for thirty pieces of silver. And they denied ever knowing him, not once, not twice, but three times.

Jesus had The Core as well. The ones who had seen the glory the Father has given Him. The ones who were one with Him, just as He and the Father are one. The ones who believed that Jesus was sent to the earth to die and rise again for the sins of the world. The ones brought into complete unity. We are The Core in the circles of Christ. We understand the pieces of His heart, and we stand by the truth, His truth, His word.

THREE MORE CS: CHARACTER, CHARISMA, AND CHEMISTRY

The worst thing you can do is mix up your circles. The people in The Crowd do not belong in The Crew; the people in The Crew do not belong in The Core. They have not earned the right to take the pieces of you reserved for the ones who have shown their allegiance to your calling and your destiny. You are like a business. If you value your business, you are not going to allow just any employee to work for you. You do background checks, review resumes, check for experience, observe the qualities that make them an added value to your stock. The way someone treats others is a good indication of how they treat you.

When creating these circles, we must know who takes our energy level and who takes our virtue level. The ones who are constantly taking are always taking because you are always giving. If all you do is give, you end up giving yourself away, all of your pieces are gone. You need to be in a certain place in your life to do that, because if helping you is hurting me then it's no help to anyone. These are energy drainers, virtue suckers. You need to analyze people and discover who they are. We must find security in our relations and our friends. When friends are secure, they don't fight over who's next as if God only has one seat.

The higher you go, the better success you have, and the more is revealed in the motives and intents of the people around you. It's critical to concretize yourself within yourself and not others around you.

> *...decide never to put a stumbling block or hindrance in the way of a brother.*
>
> –Romans 14:13

There are great achievements in your world that every single person does not deserve the right or access to know. If you flagrantly say to just anyone, "I just got a promotion on my job. I'm making $20,000 more than I used to!" to an unemployed person, you just created a stumbling block for your brother. They are now looking at you from a place of envy. If you reveal yourself to the wrong person, you turn from John the Beloved into Judas the Traitor.

You are too gifted not to be great. And you are too smart to struggle with simple battles. You can't add to people if you are not valuable, but you need to first realize that you are valuable. There are people that will take that value from you, they will take your heart. A lot of times we are hanging around people and we want them to appreciate us, but they can't appreciate us because we tend to devalue ourselves.

The circles we make should be filled with people that have these Three Cs: competence, character, and chemistry. These friends of yours in The Crowd, The Crew, and The Core, they need these Three Cs. Some of them might have degrees of competence and character; you yourself might be saying *hey I'm competent AND I have character*—chances are everyone else around you is saying the same thing about themselves, and you know full well some of them are severely lacking both competence and character.

There's nothing more frustrating than trying to hold a high concept conversation with someone who is incompetent; competence requires intelligence. Don't oversell your own intelligence, or else you reveal your own lack of competence. To determine character, you must understand the emotional capacity of the individual in question. There are some people that are emotionally broken. They cannot be effective in building relationships because they need to focus on building themselves first—that's not your job, that's their job. If you know that glass has been broken and taped back up, you're going to handle that glass differently. Your touch is softer, and that means your grasp is loose, and that means the probability of dropping that glass is that much higher. Gently lift the glass, gingerly place the glass. Don't make too much noise or the glass is going to shatter. You end up spending more time trying to figure out how to handle the glass than actually handling the glass. And when it breaks again, and it will break again, who do you think is going to be blamed? It's not the fault of the glass: it's you. The glass will only be mended after it has gone through a refiner's fire; and we have the great opportunity to come to the Great Refiner, the Lord God Almighty.

If it's snowing, you know it's not Summer. If it's time to reap the harvest, you know it's not Winter. If there are Trick-or-Treaters knocking on your door, you know it's not Spring. There are seasons people go through; you may be in Spring and everything is going right, but your brother may be in Fall and things are going to get sour really fast. You're not going to be able to speak into him effectively because he is not in your season! There will be some things you will not share with him, some pieces of yourself which you must hold back, and if he is competent enough, if he has enough character, he will understand that. That's the chemistry, that reaction when conflicting elements meet, conflicting seasons, and an explosion of understanding occurs.

You know when someone in your circle has no chemistry. I have a workout group. We've been going to the gym for two years. What makes the group successful is the chemistry we have with one another. There is nothing more frustrating than when someone has great character, graceful competence, but no chemistry. It's like when you play the black note and the white note on the piano at the same time, there's dissonance, it's not a pretty sound. You butt heads, you don't get each other's jokes. It's a bad scene. Just because someone has character and competence doesn't mean they have chemistry with you.

ONE MORE C: CADENCE

Cadence is the ability to move at the beat of the drum. If you have your own beat going, and someone has their own beat going, you don't share a cadence. This will frustrate you. You can drop your cadence and pick up theirs, but then you are not your own anymore. Your value is depreciated because you gave up the wrong piece of yourself. Sometimes you need to let people walk out their own cadence when it doesn't match yours.

When Jesus was at the end of His ministry, during the Passover Dinner, the Last Supper; He knew there was a cadence different from His own, and He called it out. "What you are about to do, do quickly," He said to one of His disciples, and Judas ran out, selling his Lord out for some silver. There was another one of His disciples that Jesus called out, He was feeling a different cadence. He told Peter he would betray Him three times. Peter denied he'd ever do that, until it happened after Jesus was arrested. Both Judas and Peter were sorry for what they'd done, but they revealed their character in different ways. Judas ended his life, in the field that was bought with his silver, with his ultimate betrayal. Peter revealed his character not by taking his life, but letting Jesus take over his life, until the end of his when it was time for him to be martyred. In his apology, he knew he wasn't worthy to die the same way as his Lord. Out of respect, and in his competence, he inverted his cross and was crucified for the sake of Jesus. Here were two traitors, in the chemistry of redemption, and they both died the death of execution. Except one remained a traitor, while the other remained a part of The Core. Whose Core are you a part of? Who are you letting come into your Core, Judas or Peter?

Jesus left Nazareth for Capernaum because that city was the port. That's where all the traffic was, the markets, the people, the rich, the poor. Your gifts, your anointing, your mantles need to be in the precise environment to grow. There's a reason you don't see any palm trees in the North East. That environment is not conducive to the palm tree's potential. The palm tree has its cadence, and the North East has its cadence, and those rhythms are different, but they thrive in Florida, where the cadence matches. A lot of us in our gifting cannot take off the way we want to take off because we're in an environment that quenches our seed, and so we don't grow. We haven't set up boundaries. We haven't drawn our circles the right way. We haven't analyzed the people around us, those who are competent, those that have character, those that have chemistry, those who march to the same beat of the drum. A goldfish can only grow so large in a small pond; once you place that goldfish in the sea, it can expand to twice its previous size. It grows in relationship to the boundaries in which it is set. It's scary moving from the pond and into the sea. But when we venture into the unknown, that place of the unfamiliar, that is where were stretched.

Boundaries, these circles of influence we draw, are important. They let us know where people can go and what people can access. I have a fence in my backyard and it separates my property from this little canal. My kids like to play in the backyard, so in order to protect what I love from danger, I need to put up a fence, draw a line in the sand, draw my circle. If you don't give certain people boundaries, even those whom you love, they are going to get hurt, and not only are they falling into the canal, you are going to end up in there with them. I'm not punishing my kids by erecting a fence, I love my kids enough to protect them from the things I know they can't handle. Place boundaries around The Crowd so they don't become The Crew. Place boundaries around The Crew so they don't become The Core. Analyze your people, understand their level of competence, character, and chemistry. If you know someone is a gossiper, don't give them information. You will get mad at them for gossiping. You can prevent your brother from stumbling.

Accept people for who they are, you can't change that. Gossipers can often be great friends, just as long as you know where the boundaries are. If you let them cross your boundary, if they invade the circle of influence you've constructed to protect yourself and the people you love, then it's on you when you get hurt.

CHAPTER 7

MANTLES, MEASURES, AND MENTORS

There is something called *the curse of knowledge.* This is the occurrence of a perceptual bias when an individual assumes that others have the background to understand what it is they are communicating. Our brains create fantastic simulations. We can predict the paths objects will take through space, like when a batter hits a 90 mph fastball to a speed of 110 mph in to the air and the right field gets right under it. We can also place ourselves in someone else's shoes and attempt to imagine their thoughts, intentions, possible actions. Without the ability to create these simulations, we would be lost in the social world. This is the core tenant of empathy, a valuable tool in dealing with people.

Often times we unconsciously create these simulations, and because of our curse of knowledge, our empathy radars are turned off. We become so self-involved by default.

This ability to fit ourselves in the shoes of others is called "theory of mind" in psychology. Understanding of the theory of mind in children is vital in the development in this theory. Heinz Wimmer and Josef Perner from the University of Salzburg first experimented using a test of false beliefs to provide ecidence about when this theory of mind emerges (Wimmer & Perner, 1983). The researchers sought whether children could pass a false belief test. They needed to understand that it was possible for other people to hold beliefs that were different to their own.

Children between the ages of 3 and 9 were told a story about a boy named Maxi. Maxi's mother brought home some chocolate to make a cake. When she gets home Maxi sees her put the chocolate into a blue cupboard. Then Maxi goes out to play. Meanwhile, his mother uses the chocolate for the cake but instead of the blue cupboard, she puts it in the green cupboard. When Maxi comes back from playing, he decides he wants some chocolate. The children in the experiment are then asked not where the chocolate is, but which cupboard Maxi will look in. The story is acted out using dolls and puppets to make the story come alive for the children. At the end of the experiment, the 3 and 4 year olds tended to fail the test by pointing to the *actual* position of the chocolate rather than *where* Maxi thought it was. They couldn't understand that although they knew where it was, Maxi didn't. The conclusion was that they were not able to at this age construct a theory of mind. The results were mixed in the 5 and 6 year olds, but mostly fell in line to hold true to the theory of mind: they pointed to the cupboard Maxi believed the chocolate was in.

Variations of the experiment were performed, but the studies showed that children outgrow the most flagrant errors produced by cognitive limitations. Adults, though, are still saddled with a version of it. We assume others understand the words we use, share the same skills we possess, and know the obscure facts that we perceive as common knowledge.

Steven Pinker, a cognitive scientist, citied a passage from an article on consciousness published in a cognitive science journal intended for wide readership (Pinker, 2015):

The slow and integrative nature of conscious perception is confirmed behaviorally by observations such as the "rabbit illusion" and its variants, where the way in which a stimulus is ultimately perceived is influenced by poststimulus events arising several hundreds of milliseconds after the original stimulus.

Despite teaching and researching in perception for almost 40 years, Pinker says he had "no idea" what the sentence was supposed to mean. He found what "the rabbit illusion" was:

The subject closes his eyes and sticks out his arm,
The experimenter taps him three times on the wrist,
three times on the elbow, three times on the shoulder,
and it feels like a continuing series of taps running up
the length of your arm, kind of like a hopping rabbit—
hence, 'the rabbit illusion.'

Upon reading this, Pinker said, "well, why didn't he just say that?"

We can't ever know what other people are thinking, even if we try really hard. The ability to empathize with others is critical in order to be rid of assumptions and escape the curse of knowledge.

A MEASUREMENT OF ASSUMPTIONS

We all have people in our lives that we engage in different circles of our relationship. Sometimes they are outside all of our circles of influence. When God gives you a direction to go, He will send someone to help you. Often we are too busy waiting on God to do something when he has sent someone to you so you can get to where you are supposed to be. People often say, "all I need is God." Yes, you do need God. God can use people to get things done. If he wants to set the Israelites free, he's going to send Moses to Pharaoh. If Moses is too tongue tied to speak effectively, he's going to send Aaron to speak on Moses' behalf.

God sends people to act as measuring sticks to get us to the next dimension. These measuring sticks are given the grace to unlock the grace hidden within us.

The word of God is the ultimate measure for our walk with the Lord. It is proficient in teaching and correction. So when you come to church and hear the word of God, it's not just the words you are hearing. You are hearing God speaking things to you and, unlocking things within you. Your pastor is a mentor in your life. He has been placed in your path to help you along the way. That's why it is important to listen to what he says when he is giving you the Word. Your pastor is not your only mentor, you do not need to only have one. Mentorship is always available to you but that does not mean it is always accessible to you. You must first maximize the relationships with those you feel have something to offer you to get you over to the next level.

Elisha maximized his relationship with Elijah. He said *wherever you go I'm going because I know if I follow that mantle, there is a measure that will fall on me.* That doesn't mean he will get the full extent of what his mentor is carrying, necessarily. God will always give the mantle that fits on your shoulders. It's not too big, it's not too small. It fits you like a suit on your wedding day.

Houses are assembled with mantles. The mantles are connected when erected so that it can stand on its own. Every church is a house, whether it's a church of worship, entrepreneurs, dreamers, or hope every church has a mantle. A spiritual mantle. You know when you are approaching a church of worship because you can feel the praise breaking out. God releases a measure of that mantle to you in that moment. It's not like the mantle your brother is getting because it fits you and you alone.

While Elisha was following everywhere Elijah went, Elisha desired the mantle Elijah had. Elijah reminded Elisha that if he sees him go, only then can he have the mantle. That is how he measured Elisha. So Elijah goes up and Elisha gets the mantle. Elisha passed all of the tests. He must have thought Elijah was just outside of his mind from time to time, but there was persistence in his pursuit which showed desire. With this mantle, Elisha didn't do all of the things Elijah did. It wasn't the same mantle. However, it was the mantle God had given him, and he did many things in the name of the Lord. How God is going to use you may not be the same way that you've seen it done. You have to blaze your own trail because that other trail has been taken already. You know where that leads. Instead, you go down the road less traveled.

To know the mantle you will get, you need to know your value. I first started preaching when I was twelve years old. That was over twenty years ago. There was this church not too long ago, I took off work so I could preach at their weekly services for a whole week straight. As a gift they gave me a clock. I figured they thought I didn't know how to tell time. I didn't value their gift because I didn't feel like they valued my gift. I assumed I would be financially compensated since I took off work. I poured myself out and my persistence did not match my reward. I couldn't have known what they were thinking, I simulated in my mind I would get paid. Thanks to this scenario, I now know to get all of the information before I extend my gifts to the body of Christ.

Know your value.

The job of a mentor is to ensure that his apprentice grows healthy. My neighbor had a tee that had gotten blown over in a storm. It was crooked, bowing closer to the earth, but it was still alive. You can grow crooked and still be alive. It takes care to straighten out a crooked tree. You peg a stake into the ground opposite the direction of the tree growth and tie a strong rope around the tree. Then attach the rope to the stake, and over time, as the tree grows taller, the crooked becomes straight.

A mentor measures how crooked we are, and he stretches us as we grow. God uses others to stretch our faith in order to show us the necessity of our ability to follow instructions. Your next level is not in who you're connected to, it's your ability to follow. Those who neglect to follow get eliminated from accessing the door of opportunity. There is weight given to a mentor. Whatever Elijah said to Elisha, Elisha said over and over again *whatever you tell me to do, that's what I'm going to do. I'm not going to leave you where you are because even though you are leading me to where I don't want to go, I trust the ending is bigger than where you are leading me right now.* This wasn't easy for Elisha. It seemed like he was being led to places that were contrary to what he wanted for himself. When God gives mantles, he doesn't give them back, they stay on the earth. The way you love the man determines the measure of the mantle you are going to get.

When Elisha died, they threw a dead man on him and the dead man was raised to life because Elisha never passed on his mantle to anyone else. We all have parents that have all these home remedies. My mother is from the islands, and they have these crazy elixirs: cut down a tree, burn it six times and mix it with tea leaves. They make no sense! You should look at these like treasures because they often are not written down. When we lose the person we lose their knowledge. The older generation have these songs they've sung in the church. They have this spirit attached to them, the mantle is just on them so strong. These songs sparked revival in the past and they move the entire room. It's got this measure of weight on it. We need to catch the mantle of the older generation so they don't get lost. We might feel like we are better than the generation before us, but God always uses each generation differently. He measures with the different end of the stick. If you continue to criticize the previous generation, you limit the opportunity to be used at the maximum capacity God wanted to use you. This older generation has been through more than you can know in your present state, and we don't see that. We assume things about them based on the glimpses we see, we forget to empathize, we forget to put on their shoes and walk around for a day. Always remember to honor those that have come before you.

I had the opportunity to serve under Reverend Gracey. He retired after 20 years in the ministry as a pastor. He had set the standard for us to do what we do and so we took a moment to honor him because honor doesn't mean I agree with everything you do. It is a position of honor that I give you in my life that says even though I disagree with you, I won't dishonor you.

How you exit is how you enter. In every aspect of life, whether it be in the job, the church, relationships, how you exit is how you enter. Your work might be hell on earth, but you are going to give two weeks notice and a resignation letter because you honor even in disagreement. You might have left your church and never told the pastor. You brag about your new pastor and you when you old one sees he asks himself when did this happen? When you have honor in your heart, you bless, you baptize you save, you preach. If you want to do ministry or you get ministered to, go back to the place you left and say, "listen, I just want to thank you for all that you've done for me." You can't go up until you go down.

My pastor and I hadn't spoken in four years. Every birthday I'd send him a check. He'd cash it and never call. No thank you. He'd never even respond. I sent him emails with the read receipt to make sure it was him that was getting it. Every birthday, every church anniversary, I'd send him a check. Never a response. It was never about the response for me, though. It was about the honor. There are things happening in my life that are only happening because even when I was wronged I still showed honor. I did everything I could to ensure that I was one to be called a man of honor. Most of you want to go up, but you can't go up because your ego is pulling you down. We all find out how heavy pride can be.

I've worked with my brother for five years. He's my real brother, we dropped the in-law a long time ago. When we worked together, there was plenty of times he disagreed with my decision making, but he never once dishonored me. He honored me even in disagreement, when he didn't like what I was saying. I'm sure there were times he went home and chewed me out. He never showed that to me. He kept a level of honor above bar. I said to him, "the level of honor you give to one is the harvest of what you receive in your own fields."

We are a generation who lack honor, and we wonder why we don't see God moving in our lives. As sure as I serve God's people in a culture of honor, I wait in anticipation to see God move.

NEXT IN LINE

What's the worst part about shopping in the supermarket? Trying to get a parking spot on a weekend morning hurts my witness for salvation. People reading the labels and their shopping carts are in the middle of the aisle. You can't pass by. Some woman wipes her nose with her hand and starts feeling how soft the oranges are. Someone spilled something? Not their problem. Walk away like nothing happened. No, the worst part about shopping in the supermarket is the line. The line of cars getting in, the line of cars getting out, the line you have to stand in to get out. We all want the line to move fast so we can leave fast. My friend thinks he has good instincts when choosing a line. He will analyze each line and then pick the line that he feels will move the fastest. I was with him this one time and we get in line. He was so sure this line would be the first one out. Lane seven though kept spitting out customers one after another. "Come on," he said. "Let's move to lane seven." So we get out of line and move to lane seven, which automatically comes to a complete halt as soon as we step in. We look on in horror as our previous lane starts moving faster than lane seven was.

Sometimes your lane isn't moving. You are stuck in line and you are waiting to be next. You see others around you moving up, they get checked out, but you're still waiting. Don't get out of line. Stay in there, your time will come. The moment you step out is the moment you prolong your time in line, your time in the waiting. Some of you are next in line and you need to check your attitude and your disposition when your name gets called. You did all the work and praying and then you let someone in the line get to you, and out of character you step out of the season God had called you to.

There was a man in the bible named Gehazi, who stepped out of line. He was the servant of Elisha, after Elijah was taken up. He was in the lane for the mantle, Elisha's mantle.

Remember, Elisha followed Elijah everywhere. He was in line to be next. He wanted the mantle. So then when he was operating in his anointing, Gehazi followed Elisha everywhere. He was the shadow of Elisha. He helped spread the message of God to the people.

There was a man named Naaman who was sick. He had leprosy, a terrible disease. It attacks the nervous system resulting in the lack of ability to feel pain. If you don't feel pain, you are going to get banged up a whole lot. If you don't know you broke your leg and you think you're just walking funny, then that leg is going to fall right off. Wounds end up untreated, and infection spreads, like gangrene. Extremities start falling off. The cartilage gets absorbed into your body, so then fingers and toes become shortened and deformed. Elisha told him to soak in the Jordan. Naaman had his reservations. He didn't want to go in that nasty water, what good could come of that? Maybe you've been somewhere in your life where you ask God for help, and he tells you what to do and instead of doing it you ask why. Naaman went to the Jordan and did what Elisha told him and he was healed. He offered Elisha gifts, a payment for services rendered. Elisha never asked for a gift, nor payment, so he refused Naaman's offering. You can't buy God's blessings. His miracles don't come with a price tag. But Gehazi chased after Naaman. He saw the riches available and accessible to him. So he chased after Naaman and took the gifts meant for the one who blessed. Elisha asked Gehazi where he had gone and Gehazi played dumb, like he didn't go anywhere. But Elisha said, "Was not my spirit with you when he got down from his chariot to meet you?" The prophet knew everything Gehazi did. He saw his greed, his action in that greed, and he cursed him with the leprosy that belonged to Naaman.

Gehazi left his mentor, and decided to take a path that wasn't meant for him when he chased down Naaman. That is exactly when he forfeited his destiny. The mantle was no longer his to bear, and instead of an anointing he received a curse. He stepped out of the line because he thought he saw a better opportunity for himself. Gehazi did what most of us do. We are so concerned about getting what's next instead of getting what's now. If Gehazi had done what he was supposed to do, he would have been next in line. He let greed, his flesh, talk him out of his inheritance, God made up His mind what he was going to give him, and it was worth more than a couple talents of silver and bundles of clothes. When you take short cuts you get cut short. Honor is a principle. Those who do not live their lives with honor will suffer the consequences of dishonor. Marriages end where honor ends. Honor is the weight given to another. You share a burden together. If you don't share that burden with someone, you carry it all yourself, and your shoulders get sore after a while. There's nothing you will respect in another person. You need that person who you are okay with going through your mail. If you don't have that kind of person, you end up being a spoiled brat. You don't get your toy at the store, then you're throwing a tantrum, shut down the whole Way-Mart. Look at aisle six everyone. They're all looking at you, the whole store. You don't have anyone in your life that will tell you the truth, and you don't rebut you just accept it. You say, "I'm like this because—" You act like you don't want that. You want breastmilk, a nurse to burp you. Do you know why your marriage isn't working? You're mean and nasty. Do you know why you're single? You're petulant. Marriage doesn't change who you are, it magnifies who you are. We live in a world where we point the finger at everyone but ourselves, just for the satisfaction. But you'll never be truly satisfied.

Many people chase the dollar but not the assignment. Your assignment may not pay you, but God makes up for that. When he puts you on something, he's going to make sure he takes care of you. Just like if he cuts you, you'll bleed but he will sew you back up. Often times God will cut a person and they'll jump off the physician's table. I could have chased the dollar, but I stayed with my assignment. I had no business buying a house, but God provided financial providence to put a roof over my head. This man with holes in his jeans that were too tight for him to be wearing came up to me and asked if I was getting married. I said yes. He told me he wanted to sell me his house. You only had to take one look at this guy to know his house was on the wrong side of town. He got out of an 87 Ford Escort. The driver's side door didn't work, he had to hop in and out of the window. Be honest, everyone knows if someone offers you a house, you look at their car to get an idea of who you are dealing with.

He tells me, though, that he knows I work at a church, that I don't make a lot of money. He invites me to the house, and since I have nothing to lose, I check it out. This house that he owned and wanted to sell me, it was worth $245,000. It was in the neighborhood I wanted to live in: Sawmill. I found out this man owned properties all over the country. This wasn't some transient pulling one over on me, this was a legitimate tycoon opening a door of opportunity. He let me have that house for a fraction of what it was worth. I assumed something about this man because of my curse of knowledge. My previous experiences influenced my perception of projected events. I walked out what God had for me, I stayed in line and He blessed me with the desires of my heart.

In relationships you must always measure your capacity and willingness to help others help themselves. Jesus in his own home town could not perform the miracles in the lives of the people because he was known as the Carpenter. They relegated his position of status based on their perceptual bias. Their curse of knowledge was the measure of his efficacy. In the next town over, the woman with the issue of blood measured Jesus as the messiah, as a healer, and her measurement of his ability effected (affected?) how she received a miracle. How someone sees you, how they measure you, often determines how you can mentor them into a new season.

Jesus was a mentor to his disciples in an intimate way. Elizabeth mentored Mary. It wasn't just about Elija and Elisha. The whole bible is filled with these examples. These were people who were willing to be vulnerable, not just teaching the word as if you were a follower of the crow. They showed their scars and their humanity. Jesus revealed to them who he was when he was weeping, his transfiguration on the mountain top, bringing them into a show and tell opportunity to see how miracles happen: these are the signs of mentorship. Mentors don't work at a distance, they work with you and show you value in lessons once they are gone. Elisha remember the healing virtue and miracles. When Jesus went away to minister was born, Mary was able to go back to those months when she lived under the tutelage of Elizabeth. Especially Naomi sharing to Ruth not just her blessings but her bitterness and pain. When Ruth moved on in her own life and married, she was able to take those nuggets of pain and use them for purpose. Mentors share their pain, their sorrow, their tears because you can benefit more from it than they can. They are always willing to share the truth, no matter how much it hurts.

Mentorship is the assessment of the capacity within another to handle the vulnerability within. It's only when you are most vulnerable that your mantle can be passed down, your legacy. And if you are working under a mentorship, then your vulnerability is amplified because when it comes time for you take what is yours, the measure by which you were tested is the measure by which you will test. The sorrows of yesterday will become the joys of tomorrow.

BIBLIOGRAPHY

Wimmer, H., & Perner, J. (1983). Beliefs about beliefs: representation and constraining function of wrong beliefs in young children's understanding of deception. Cognition, 13(1), 103-28.

"Chapter 3: The Curse of Knowledge." The Sense of Style the Thinking Person's Guide to Writing in the 21st Century, by Steven Pinker, Penguin Books, 2015.

Pastor David S. Jacques, known to many as "Pastor David", is a passionate spiritual leader who is dedicated to preaching the Gospel to the Kingdom of God. Through a respectable understanding of context and culture, Pastor David helps bridge the gap between the biblical text and the modern day hearer. As founder and senior pastor of The Kingdom Church (TKC) in Orlando, Florida, Pastor David's focus is on Enlightening, Empowering and Encouraging believers and unbelievers alike.

Actively serving in ministry since the tender age of 12, Pastor David's first ministerial role came when he served as director for the Youth and Young Adult Ministry at First Haitian Baptist Church of Orlando. At the age of 17, Pastor David continued to be a blessing when he launched Scriptural Warfare, an inner-city Bible study in the Carver Shores neighborhood, in West Orlando, Florida. This inner-city program was later merged with and continued at New Destiny Christian Center, under the late Pastor Zachery Tims, where he also served as young adult minister.

Pastor David is a firm believer in the importance of receiving an education and accomplished many academic achievements throughout his life. As a graduate of Dr. Phillips High School, Pastor David was in the Center for International Studies (CIS) Magnet Program. He currently holds a Bachelor of Science Degree in Business Management from the University of Phoenix. He also received his Associate of Arts Degree, while minoring in Biblical Studies from Belhaven College. He is currently pursuing his Master's Degree. He is an alumnus of Princeton Theological Seminary certificate program, Yale Divinity certificate program, and Black Theological Leadership Institute. He is a licensed commercial real estate agent and owns several entrepreneurial businesses.

Pastor David's many accomplishments are of no surprise to his family and friends. When his mother was three months pregnant with him, she recalls a prophetic dream in which the Lord told her, "This child will become a pastor." As young as seven her dream had begun to manifest. Pastor David was observed preaching to empty chairs as well as to friends on the basketball court. Today the Boston native continues to fulfill the legacy spoken of him in his mother's womb.

Pastor David is the proud husband of Karen Jacques. They have four beautiful children: David, Destini, Desiree, and Devon. Pastor David is a young man reaching destiny and fulfilling purpose all for the glory of God.

Contact page

Pastor David S. Jacques
1400 N. Nowell St Orlando, FL 32808

Instagram: pdsj_tkc
Facebook: www.facebook.com/pdsjtkc or fb.me/pdsjtkc

www.ingramcontent.com/pod-product-compliance
Lightning Source LLC
Chambersburg PA
CBHW031514040426
42445CB00009B/228